Software Requirements
Using the Unified Process

ISBN 0-13-096972-9

90000

9 790130 969728

Software Requirements Using the Unified Process

A Practical Approach

DANIEL R. WINDLE

L. RENE ABREO

PRENTICE HALL PTR
UPPER SADDLE RIVER, NJ 07458
WWW.PHPTR.COM

Library of Congress Cataloging-in-Publication Data

Windle, Daniel R.
  Software requirements using the unified process: a practical approach/Daniel R.
  Windle, L. Rene Abreo.
      p. cm.
  Includes bibliographical references and index.
  ISBN 0-13-096972-9
  1. Computer software—Development. 2. Software engineering. I. Abreo, L. Rene. II.
  Title.
  QA76.76.D47 W555 2002
  005.1—dc21   2002075285

Editorial/production supervision: *June Bonnell*
Composition: *Aurelia Scharnhorst*
Cover design director: *Jerry Votta*
Cover design: *Nina Scuderi*
Manufacturing manager: *Alexis R. Heydt-Long*
Executive editor: *Paul Petralia*
Editorial assistant: *Richard Winkler*
Marketing manager: *Debby vanDijk*

© 2003 Pearson Education, Inc.
Publishing as Prentice Hall PTR
Upper Saddle River, New Jersey 07458

Prentice Hall books are widely used by corporations and government agencies for training, marketing, and resale.
For information regarding corporate and government bulk discounts please contact:
Corporate and Government Sales (800) 382-3419 or corpsales@pearsontechgroup.com

Company and product names mentioned herein are the trademarks or registered trademarks of their respective owners.

Printed in the United States of America
10   9   8   7   6   5   4   3   2   1

ISBN 0-13-096972-9

Pearson Education LTD.
Pearson Education Australia PTY, Limited
Pearson Education Singapore, Pte. Ltd.
Pearson Education North Asia Ltd.
Pearson Education Canada, Ltd.
Pearson Educación de Mexico, S.A. de C.V.
Pearson Education—Japan
Pearson Education Malaysia, Pte. Ltd.

Contents

CHAPTER 7
Using Activity Diagrams to Represent Use Cases   57

CHAPTER 8
Writing Use Cases   67

CHAPTER 9
Using Storyboards to Validate the Use Cases   77

Preface

We intend that this book provide you with a practical approach to gathering, analyzing, specifying, and managing software requirements throughout the software's life cycle.

If you are an analyst responsible for specifying requirements from which software systems are built, we think you will find a straightforward and effective approach to meeting the demands of the users you work with and the developers and testers you deliver specifications to.

If you are a developer responsible for building software systems from requirements specifications, we think you will find an effective way to communicate all software requirements in a coherent and easy-to-follow manner.

If you are a tester responsible for testing software systems from a specification, we think you'll find that the specifications described in this book provide a complete and clear control flow model of the entire system, allowing you to systematically develop tests. We also believe you will find that the requirements artifacts described in this book will allow you to learn a new system quickly and thoroughly.

If you are a manager of software development or testing, we think you will find that the establishment and maintenance of requirements artifacts will ensure that you can always quickly bring new people up to speed on your systems. We also believe you will find a practical approach to shortening the time it takes to specify software requirements while maintaining your organization's intellectual property.

Acknowledgments

First, we would like to thank our wives, Kathleen Windle and Sandi Abreo, and our children—Tasha Windle, Cynthia Windle, Michael Abreo, and Alexandra Abreo—for their understanding and patience as we embarked on this endeavor.

We would also like to thank our colleagues at the Securities Industry Automation Corporation in New York City who helped with reviews of this book, in particular, Mark Lewis and Alex Ciccotelli, who generously gave of their time. We would like to specifically thank Charles Bowman for setting us on the path to writing this book.

Software Requirements
Using the Unified Process

Introducing Good Requirements

The Importance of Good Requirements

Rationale for Good Requirements

Real-world systems are built every day and based on skimpy requirements. We know this because most of us have been on projects where the requirements change daily. Sometimes these changes are due to the customer changing his mind. More often, these changes are due to clarifications of the software requirements that come late in the project. Anyone responsible for the maintenance of one or more significant projects has also experienced the effects of building systems with skimpy requirements. Many of us have struggled with reliance on single individuals for knowledge about what a system does. Some of us have been that individual struggling to remember all the interdependencies among the requirements we are being asked to change to implement a particular release. The approach described in this book is a practical approach to developing software requirements. We have successfully delivered a significant number of systems by using this process and the resulting artifacts. These systems have ranged from defense command and control systems to web systems to financial transaction processing systems. We have also recovered the requirements from existing systems by using this process to alleviate the reliance on individuals and to improve the speed and quality of maintenance activities.

Requirements tell you the features a system must have as well as what the software must do to deliver those features. This is a significant aspect of requirements: they possess a dual nature. Features represent user requirements. What the software does represents software requirements. There is a large gap between user requirements and software requirements. The artifacts and process described in this book will help you fill that gap. You work with the user to determine what features the system must have. From this feature set, you must derive a set of components that can deliver those features. These components and their relationship to each other lead you to a software architecture. This architecture tells you what the software must do. The user requirements come from describing the user's interaction with the system. You derive the software requirements during analysis by mapping the user requirements onto the software architecture.

Requirements are normally the work of a requirements analyst. While the dual nature of requirements may lead an analyst to specialize in user requirements or software requirements, generally an analyst serves two customers. The first is the user of the system. The second is the developer of the system who must design a system to meet the specified requirements.

The analyst serves another customer indirectly. This customer is the organization. What a system does for which user is critical knowledge for the organization. The value a software organization brings to its customers is an understanding of how the software supports the business. Customers understand their business. Users understand how they use the software to work in the business. However, it is usually only the software professionals that understand what the software does to support the business. Therefore, good requirements are necessary to ensure that you build the right system and also to ensure that the organization safely stores the intellectual capital it possesses.

Approach to Good Requirements

How many times have you heard the phrase "the user does not know what he wants"? This phrase is most often wrong. The user often has an idea of what he wants—he just does not know the specifics. There may be many reasons for this. One reason may be that the user does not know what is possible. Another reason may be that the user is considering the software from a single point of view. It is up to the analyst to understand what the user wants, communicate what is possible, and then specify what the user wants and exactly what the software must do.

To perform this task, the analyst must be able to move forward with the requirements work in the context of providing feedback to the user and incorporating that feedback into a growing body of knowledge. A practical approach to address these challenges is to use a process that builds knowledge incrementally. At the same time, this practical approach would also augment this process with a structure that saves, relates, and communicates this information coherently. This structure must also help the analyst keep this information consistent.

The process described in this book presents a disciplined approach. It explicitly integrates use cases with various models and the models with the requirements specification. The use cases represent the user requirements. The Software Requirements Specification represents the software requirements. The models provide the analyst with the tools to ensure that user requirements are represented by and consistent with the software requirements.

Benefits of Good Requirements

Good requirements provide many benefits. These benefits impact development and productivity, testing and quality, and the organization. You will enjoy these benefits during the development of new systems as well as during maintenance of existing systems.

Impact of Good Requirements on Development and Productivity

The most visible benefit to this process is faster and higher-quality requirements analysis. A full set of requirements allows an analyst to identify all conflicts between user requirements up front. Identifying all unanswered questions and getting answers to those questions early saves the time and effort spent in building the wrong product and the time and effort spent reworking the products that were based on the poor requirements. A good set of requirements also represents a single source of a system's requirements. This means that all the functions a system performs to meet a set of user needs can be found in one place.

A good set of requirements provides a foundation to begin design. The analyst's two primary customers speak two different languages. The user is interested in seeing the business from an automated point of view. The developer wants to understand the structure and dynamic behavior of the software to ensure that the design accomplishes what the user wants. A good set of requirements provides a direct mapping from the requirements as expressed in the language of the user to the requirements as expressed in the language of the developer.

Impact of Good Requirements on Testing and Quality

A good set of requirements helps decrease a new team member's learning curve. Ideally, a good set of requirements provides three views: an abstract view from the user's eyes, a structural view from a software architect's eyes, and a dynamic view from the developer's eyes. A new team member can then quickly learn to use the system while at the same time understanding the structure of the software. With the big picture firmly in place, a new team member can use a good set of requirements to delve into specifics without losing perspective.

A good set of requirements also facilitates faster and more systematic testing. The tester can learn the system quickly, much as a new team member would. The tester can then build test cases from the user's point of view to organize his approach operationally. However, a good set of requirements helps the tester understand what the system must do under what conditions to fulfill the user requirements. A good set of requirements must allow the tester to understand and test all the conditions under which the user will operate the system.

Impact of Good Requirements on the Organization

Finally, a good set of requirements provides a safe store of a company's intellectual property. Many software functions are easy to duplicate. However, it is almost impossible to understand the intricacies of the most complex software systems. This situation can be further exacerbated with changes introduced over time. Building and maintaining the software becomes incredibly expensive and error prone if you cannot understand the full set of requirements.

Identification of a Good Requirement

The IEEE, in the standard for Software Requirements Specification, identifies a good requirement as correct, unambiguous, verifiable, and traceable. The IEEE also identifies a good set of requirements as complete, consistent, and modifiable. The next chapter explores each of these characteristics in detail. The process described in this book helps ensure that requirements meet these characteristics.

Characteristics of Good Requirements

2

Good requirements exhibit a known collection of characteristics both individually and as a set. We first discuss the desirable characteristics of individual requirements as well as those of a set of requirements. Additionally, we discuss the properties that a good set of requirements should possess to ensure that we communicate well with all readers of the requirements. We next discuss the use of a specific language for writing requirements to help reduce ambiguity and to help us manage a set of requirements effectively. Finally, we state the importance of effectively communicating the content of the requirement set.

Characteristics of a Good Requirement

We need each requirement to exhibit certain characteristics. These characteristics help us produce a set of requirements that are unambiguous, verifiable, deterministic, traceable, and correct. Of these characteristics, ambiguity may be the most problematic.

Ambiguity Considerations

Ambiguity is defined as uncertainty because of obscurity or indistinctness. The development and use of good requirements require good communication with users, developers, and testers. Ambiguity makes good communication difficult if not impossible. When we write requirements, we must ensure that we understand users' needs. We must, therefore, write requirements such that users readily discern any misconceptions we might have. Next, we need to effectively communicate user needs to the software developers and testers. Everyone should have the same understanding of the requirements so that we have customers with the right expectations of our systems, developers that understand what to build, and testers prepared to test the right things. To reduce ambiguity in our requirements, we need to understand where ambiguity comes from and what we might do to eliminate or reduce it.

Ambiguity arises when we write about requirements without considering how others might interpret what we have written. While this makes it sound like reducing ambiguity is easy, it is not nearly as easy as it sounds. The English language is full of traps that can lead to ambiguity. Most words in our English dictionary have a number of meanings. Pronouns can also lead to ambiguity when their antecedents are not clear. Another cause of ambiguity is the assumption that your knowledge about a subject is common knowledge. Acronyms can lead to ambiguity. As you can see, there are many ways to introduce ambiguity and the above list is not exhaustive.

Here's an example of how the pronoun "it" can make a requirement ambiguous.

The system shall allow only five valid dependent records and insurance programs; it must include the oldest.

It is not clear whether the system must keep the oldest dependent record or the oldest insurance program. Of course, that raises another problem. Each requirement should only talk about one subject. Including multiple subjects in a single requirement can lead to ambiguity and make the requirements set harder to maintain when things start changing. We might change the requirement to read:

The system shall allow only five valid dependent records.

The system shall include a record for the oldest dependent in the set of dependent records.

The system shall include any associated insurance program within a dependent record.

This set of requirements is less ambiguous than the single requirement from which these three requirements were taken.

Often, each subject area has its own set of common acronyms. People that work in these areas use the acronyms as if they are common knowledge. Here is an example.

The system shall build and transmit new record messages to the DOT.

Here it is important to ensure that DOT appears in the glossary. If we are interconnected with multiple systems and one is the Department of Transportation and another is the Data Originated Transform system, people are going to have problems determining where the record is sent.

Not being specific enough can lead to ambiguity. Here's an example.

The system will make corrections to the record where possible.

This requirement needs to be much more specific. Here is a list of questions that jump to mind. What makes a record require corrections? Is this a single-field validation or are combinations of fields also validated? What corrections will the system automatically make? When will the corrections be made? What happens to records that cannot be automatically corrected? You might come up with additional questions to clarify this requirement.

You have only to read a requirements specification with an eye toward ambiguity and you are likely to be surprised at how many ambiguous requirements you will find. There are a number of formal methods and numerous modeling techniques that significantly reduce or eliminate ambiguity. We examine three of them. There are also formal specification languages that reduce ambiguity; we look at a specification language based on predicate logic named "Z," pronounced Zed. First, though, we examine the modeling languages.

Modeling Languages   The modeling languages place the requirements in pictures to help us isolate the requirements in a way that allows us to effectively analyze them and minimize ambiguity. We focus first on Finite State Machines, then we look at Petri Nets, and finally Integrated Definition Language (IDEF) for Functional Modeling, or IDEF0.

The first modeling language we discuss is the Finite State Machine. A Finite State Machine is represented graphically in a State Transition Diagram (see Chapter 12). The State Transition Diagram models the system by using nodes to represent a given state, and arrows from one node to another identify transitions from one state to another. These arrows are activated when some event occurs that transitions the machine from one state to another. Normally, the system takes some actions during the transition. State Transition Diagrams are powerful tools for describing a system in a complete, concise, and unambiguous manner, but their use raises some problems.

State Transition Diagrams are great for describing how systems move from one state to another. However, when many types of events that do not change the system state occur, the diagrams can become confusing and hard to follow. State Transition Diagrams also suffer from state explosion phenomenon. Complex systems can have so many events and states that the diagrams become unwieldy. It is also difficult to model concurrent processes in State Transition Diagrams. Petri Nets were developed to address the concurrency issue

The second modeling language, Petri Nets, builds a type of State Transition Diagram that can represent concurrent tasks. Concurrent tasks must be synchronized to ensure that shared data is not accessed in ways that could adversely affect the system and to ensure that the system does not become deadlocked. For example, a system may become deadlocked when task1 is holding resource1 until task2 provides some input, but task2 is waiting for resource1 to determine if there is any input for task1. Petri Nets let the analyst view the various synchronization issues graphically. Like State Transition Diagrams, Petri Nets are a valuable way to model certain problems in a system.

Although Petri Nets solve the concurrency issue, they still suffer from many of the same problems as State Transition Diagrams. Petri Nets may still have too many events in a single state or too many states to effectively model. Later, when we look at Activity Diagrams, you will see that they are not as formal as Petri Nets and not as robust. Nevertheless, we believe you can use Activity Diagrams effectively to model parts of the system in which shared resources and deadlock could be a problem.

The third modeling language, IDEF0, is a government-developed standard for modeling functional requirements. IDEF represents a family of modeling languages for representing different aspects of a system. IDEF0 combines graphics and text to describe the functional system requirements. IDEF0 describes systems through a hierarchical series of diagrams.

Each diagram in an IDEF0 model consists of boxes and arrows. Each box represents a function of the system and is named with a verb or verb phrase. For example, a box might be named "Find Valid Orders." The arrows repre-

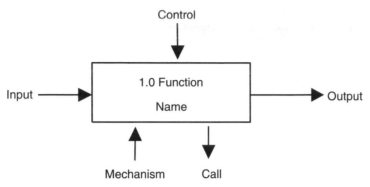

FIGURE 2.1
Integrated Definition Language Level 0

sent data or objects that are used or transformed by the function. Arrows are named with a noun or noun phrase. For example, an arrow might be named "Open Orders." Arrows entering the box from the left represent inputs to the function. Arrows entering the box from the top represent control information. Arrows leaving the box from the right represent output data. Arrows on the bottom of the box pointing toward the box represent mechanisms, and arrows on the bottom of the box pointing away from the box represent calls. Mechanisms and calls tie the model together. Functions are called by other functions through a mechanism. A specific function would call another function by using the call. Each box is numbered to refer to another diagram that shows even more detail of the function. Figure 2.1 illustrates the notation.

IDEF0 is an effective modeling language and can be used in conjunction with other IDEF models to obtain different views of the system. The IDEF0 model allows the user to view the system from different levels of abstraction. The user can view the system at a high level and then penetrate the model to examine the details of a specific function. IDEF0 modeling is an effective tool for structured analysis. However, the Unified Modeling Language better supports the object-oriented process described in this book.

The Z Specification Language   The Z language uses set theory, predicate logic, and relationships and functions to communicate requirements. When used properly, these elements of discrete mathematics allow a precise definition of each requirement and allow each requirement to be fully and completely tested mathematically. We would expect to be able to determine the outcome of a computation given the input and conditions of the system. Although Z is a powerful language for reducing ambiguity, it is difficult to learn and effectively employ. We believe we can achieve the same goals by using structured English in our specifications.

As you can see from the brief review of modeling and specification languages, significant effort has been expended trying to reduce ambiguity. We make use of this knowledge by applying elements of this work where appropriate within our process.

Verifiability Considerations

A requirement is verifiable if it can be fully testable by reasonable means. Each requirement must be verifiable to allow developers to ensure that the software they build will meet the set of requirements. Testers will base their test on the requirements set as well. They look to design tests to verify that the system works properly, handles exception conditions properly, and enforces various ranges for data sets. These goals require that each requirement be tested for correct implementation.

Here is a classic example of an unverifiable requirement.

The system will be user friendly.

There is no way to test to determine if the system is user friendly since it is only a concept. The requirement might say,

All functions must be reachable with a maximum of three keystrokes or three mouse clicks.

This requirement is verifiable.

Another example of a requirement that is not verifiable is

The employee identifier must be within a valid range.

Since the range is not defined, the requirement is not verifiable. We could restate the requirement as

The employee identifier shall be an integer inclusively in the range of 1–32,000.

This requirement is verifiable, though we would need a number of test cases to verify it.

Deterministic Considerations

Each requirement must also be deterministic so that everyone will know what the system should do in all possible cases. This means that whenever we use a conditional statement, we understand what will occur when the condition is met and what will occur if the condition is not met. Sometimes we use two different requirements to handle conditional actions. For example, we might define a requirement that specifies how to handle successfully meeting the condition and a separate requirement for not meeting the condition. Here is an example of a requirement that is not deterministic.

The system shall send new records to system X every five minutes.

This requirement is not deterministic because it does not specify what to do if no new records are received in a five-minute period. Should we send a message to specify that there are no new records or send no message at all? Perhaps we could reword the requirement as follows.

If any new messages have been received since the last transmission to system X and the five-minute timer has expired, the system shall transmit the new records to system X.

Here we are clearer about when our system will transmit new records to system X. Have we given enough information to ensure that this requirement is deterministic? Or do we need to add the following requirement?

If no new records have been received in the specified period, no action is taken.

Traceability Considerations

The next attribute we want each requirement to exhibit is traceability. Let us look at two types of requirements: user requirements and software requirements. Each of these requirements sets will be traceable to the next. Each software requirement should be uniquely identified so that it can be traced through design, implementation, and testing. This level of traceability helps ensure that each requirement is properly implemented and tested.

Having this traceability will also help us maintain the system. Whenever we need to change or remove a requirement, we will be able to quickly determine the parts of the design and implementation that support the requirement. We will also be able to identify the test cases that are used to verify the requirement.

Correctness Considerations

The last characteristic each requirement must exhibit is correctness. A requirement is correct if it accurately states a function that the system must provide. Therefore, a set of requirements is correct if each requirement is correct. We must map requirements from the user requirements to the software requirements in a manner that allows us to ensure that each requirement is correct.

Characteristics of a Good Set of Requirements _____

In addition to the characteristics we want individual requirements to exhibit, a number of other characteristics apply to our set of requirements. The set of requirements must be complete, consistent, and modifiable. These characteristics help us ensure that we deliver a quality system that we can maintain.

The first of these characteristics is completeness. Our requirements set is complete if we have captured everything the system must do to work appropriately to meet customers' expectations. This includes all functional and nonfunctional requirements. The majority of this book focuses on the functional requirements, but you must also address nonfunctional requirements. We use a template for the Software Requirements Specification to help us focus on the nonfunctional requirements. The nonfunctional requirements focus on issues like throughput, capacity, and other attributes our system must possess. To have a complete requirements set we must also consider the constraints on the system. These constraints include regulatory policies, hardware limitations, and other items that limit our design choices.

In the real world, software systems change often. Our requirements set needs to be as modifiable as possible. We must build a requirements set that is modular, relatively straightforward, and easy to change. We apply techniques throughout this process that allow us to realize these characteristics in our requirements set. We look in depth at the change process in Chapter 17.

Language of Good Requirements_____

In this book, we use specific language to express our requirements. We chose this language for two main reasons. First, we believe this language helps reduce ambiguity. Second, we use a keyword that makes it clear when we are stating a software requirement. The keyword in our language is "shall," which we express in three ways: "The system shall"; "The system shall require"; and "The system shall allow." This language centers on requirements and makes clear what the system will do.

Next, we look at an example of each of the three variations. The following requirement expresses functions the system must perform.

The system shall transmit all messages by using protocol X.

The next requirement expresses functions the system provides to external actors.

The system shall require the user to enter the last name of new employees.

The last example illustrates how we specify choices the system gives external actors.

The system shall allow the user to delete records that have not been confirmed.

We use the preceding three types of statements to specify all the requirements for our software. They may sound awkward at first, but the keyword helps us reduce ambiguity and makes it obvious when we are specifying a requirement.

Communicability of Good Requirements _____

The communicability of the requirements set is important to implementing a good system. Developing a complete and correct set of requirements will not serve its purpose if the people expected to build, test, and deploy the system do not clearly understand the requirements. Throughout this book we focus on how to communicate requirements to everyone who needs to understand them. We use different methods of communication and a number of different views of the system to ensure that we can communicate the requirements set.

We believe we can only develop excellent software if we can effectively and efficiently capture the software requirements that reflect the right characteristics. The requirements must be unambiguous, verifiable, deterministic, traceable throughout the development and maintenance processes, correct, consistent, complete, and modifiable. The more our requirements exhibit these characteristics, the more likely we are to be successful in delivering software that gets the job done.

Overview of the Artifacts and the Process

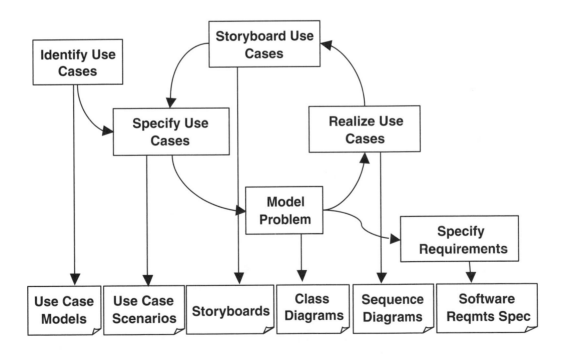

3

Introduction to the Artifacts

You can think of the requirements artifacts as those things you create as a result of the process of developing and managing requirements. Each artifact serves a particular purpose for understanding and communicating either the user requirements or the software requirements. Additionally, the artifacts relate to each other in a manner that minimizes inconsistencies. Therefore, each artifact provides a view of the full set of requirements. The set of artifacts ensures that these views do not conflict with one another. Figure 3.1 illustrates the overall architecture of the requirements artifacts. We use the diagram in Figure 3.1 throughout the book with the appropriate artifacts highlighted to provide context to the upcoming discussion.

Each artifact serves a specific purpose and results from an activity in the process. The analysis model is the primary point of reference. The analysis model contains use case models, sequence diagrams, class diagrams, state diagrams, and activity diagrams.

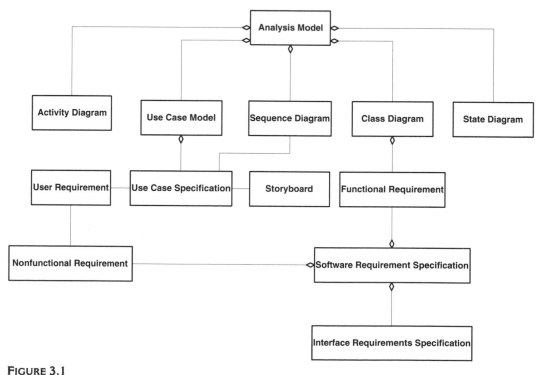

FIGURE 3.1

Requirements artifacts

The use case models represent the use cases. A use case model contains actors and use case diagrams. A use case specification describes each use case diagram (see Chapter 6). The use case specifications are the detailed description of how the user interacts with the system to achieve a specific goal (see Chapter 7). Storyboards are a series of pictures that tell the story of what occurs, from the perspective of the user, during a use case. Each use case specification has one or more storyboards (see Chapter 9). The set of use case specifications must meet all the requirements that describe what the user needs the system to do. The User Requirements are not a specific artifact we produce but are included in multiple artifacts (see Chapters 4 and 5).

The Analysis Model also contains one or more Class Diagrams. The Class Diagrams show the entities that need to work together to ensure that our system realizes each use case specification. The Class Diagram contains the functional requirements of the software. Each class possesses attributes and operations. Together, these represent the responsibilities of the class within the system. Through the analysis process, we can ensure that if objects of each class fulfill their responsibilities in collaboration with objects of the other classes in the model, then the analysis model provides a basis on which to design a system that will meet all the user requirements (see Chapters 10 and 11).

The Analysis Model also contains one or more Sequence Diagrams. Sequence Diagrams show how objects of classes in the Class Diagram collaborate to realize a use case. Each use case specification is related to one or more sequence diagrams (see Chapter 13).

The Analysis Model also contains state diagrams (see Chapter 12) and activity diagrams (see Chapter 7). Both diagrams are an aid to understanding complex issues with classes, use cases, or major aspects of the system as a whole.

The Software Requirements Specification (SRS) is the final artifact of the requirements development process. The SRS contains the specification of the functional requirements for each class in the class diagram. The SRS specifies allowable and default values for each attribute. It also specifies each operation in terms of the activities the class performs given the state of the system and the dependencies between operations as represented in the sequence diagrams (see Chapter 14). In addition to the functional requirements, the SRS contains the nonfunctional requirements. Finally, the SRS contains a specification of the interfaces to the system. However, to reduce the complexity of the SRS, our approach specifies these interfaces in an Interface Requirements Specification (IRS) (see Chapter 15).

Introduction to the Process

The process we describe is a tailored version of the Unified Process for Software Development (Jacobson et al., 1999). We have found it extremely useful for developing critical software systems in a variety of domains. We have even used the process to describe existing systems where the requirements had long been overrun by rapid delivery of incremental functionality.

The requirements engineering process consists of activities for developing requirements and managing changes to those requirements. We gather requirements by studying the user's environment, interviewing users, and learning the functionality of any existing systems. The results are specified in use cases as user requirements. We next analyze the user requirements through an analysis model that describes the entities in the user's environment and their relationships. Analysis involves building the class diagram and using sequence diagrams to realize every use case in the diagram. Once all use cases are realized in the class diagram, we build storyboards to validate the use cases with the user. After making appropriate adjustments, we specify the requirements represented by the classes, attributes, methods, and relationships from the class diagram in a Software Requirements Specification. Finally, we describe how to build use-case-driven, specification-based test cases to ensure that the software meets the requirements.

Often, the steps of the process happen concurrently. However, it is useful to discuss the process as though one step happens after another. This sequential description of the process shows the following processes:

1. How the artifacts flow into one another.
2. How you use the artifacts you have at any time to build the next artifact.
3. How you use the artifacts you have already built as a framework into which you put answers you find in later steps of the process.
4. How you use the artifacts to verify, from different yet consistent views, that your requirements are correct.

This process has three characteristics that make it effective. First, you always know what you just did. Second, you always know what to do next. Third, you have a framework within which to capture what you learn as you iterate. For example, if you have just accomplished an update to the use cases, you will need to revisit the analysis model to determine whether changes are required. This effort will include analysis of the sequence diagrams to ensure that the class diagram supports the changes to the use cases. You will then need to update the Software Requirements Specification to reflect any changes in the class diagram. This example highlights the iterative nature of the process.

Iterative Nature of the Process

The requirements process we use is iterative. You perform a sequence of operations repeatedly to produce results that get you closer to the desired state. New learning requires you to modify the requirements artifacts. You learn either as a result of analysis or user feedback. The work is frequently incremental. You may plan the requirements effort such that you deliver increments of the specification according to the user's priorities. In our process, incremental work differs from iteration. Iteration requires you to perform the same tasks on the same artifacts with the goal of creating and developing correct artifacts. A couple of examples should help illuminate this issue.

Suppose you know a set of use cases. That is, you know the user wants to achieve certain goals with this system. You describe the actors, you model the use cases, and you specify the use cases. You analyze the user requirements and discover that two goals cannot be achieved unless one of the use cases is modified. At this point, you have a version of the use cases and a version of the analysis model. You record the issues and present them to the user. The user understands your concern and makes a decision. In the next iteration, you modify the use cases and, as a result of another run through the analysis, you modify the analysis model. At the end of this iteration, the user better understands what he wants and you have a better set of use cases and a better analysis model.

In contrast, the way we describe incremental work is closer to the concept of "divide and conquer." Suppose you have 80 use cases to analyze. After reviewing the use cases, you come to the conclusion that about ten of them are incredibly complex, perhaps because they collaborate across almost all business entities in your class diagram, and the rest are fairly straightforward. You first produce an increment of the ten complex use cases. At this point, you have a version of the use cases and an analysis model that supports those use cases. For scheduling purposes, you divide the remaining use cases into two increments of 35 use cases each. As you repeat the activities of specifying the use cases and analyzing them, you update the use cases and the analysis model.

In this sense, the process we use is truly iterative and incremental. What you know and what is represented in the use cases and the analysis model starts out small. Iteration through the activities of the process results in

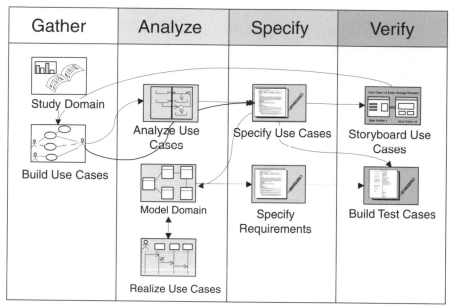

FIGURE 3.2
Process overview

increasingly more correct requirements. Incremental releases of the artifacts allow you to grow the artifacts to the full set of requirements. Iteration and incremental growth, along with a framework consisting of the use cases and the analysis model, make for quick accumulation of knowledge.

Process Flow

Figure 3.2 shows the activities of the process organized by phase. The phases include gathering, analyzing, specifying, and validating the requirements. We discuss each phase in turn.

Gathering requirements involves studying the user's environment, interviewing potential users, and documenting the results in use case models. If you are lucky, there is an existing system that the user wants to replace or incorporate into the system you are building. If this is the case, there is something for you to study. What do you do if there is no system? What do you do if the user is really starting from scratch? Here is a simple approach that has worked well:

1. *Study, study, study.* Study the business the system will support, the process the system will automate, and the rules or regulations that govern

the area of the business that the system will automate. We discuss in Chapter 4 what you should look for and how to use that information.

2. *Interview the customer and the user.* We separate the customer and the user: since you get different types of requirements from each, you should treat them separately. The user makes use of the system you develop. The customer pays for the system. Sometimes these are the same people. Most often we find they are not. Users will tell you what they want to do with the system. Customers will tell you what they want the system to cost, what they want the system to look like, and when it should be available. Hold a preliminary interview in which you use context-free questions or structured brainstorming techniques. When you get a good handle on the boundaries of the system, hold more-focused interviews to find the specifics of what users want to do with the system.

3. *Develop a use case model and the use case scenarios.* There was a time when we believed the use case model was not very useful. We are now big advocates of use case models. What seemed to be a simple set of diagrams that restated the obvious has turned into an extremely useful tool. The use case model shows you, at a glance, which actor can trigger which use case. Therefore, the process requires you to develop a use case model to go with the use case specifications. We discuss how to model the use cases in Chapter 6. We discuss how to detail the use case specifications in Chapter 8.

Analyzing the requirements involves determining the significant components of the software you are building and placing them in a class diagram. You then allocate requirements to each of those classes, using sequence diagrams to ensure that the software meets all the users' requirements. The value provided by the analysis model cannot be overstated. You will find errors in your requirements work. You will find that you missed key requirements. You will need to make changes even before you finish the requirements. The analysis model provides a framework for removing the duplication found in the use cases. It provides a framework for isolating the inevitable inconsistencies. Finally, it provides a framework into which you put the answers to issues and questions once you find them. The activities of this phase follow.

1. *Analyze use cases.* Full understanding of the user requirements represented by the use cases may require analysis. The process provides for Activity Diagrams (see Chapter 7) that show the flow of activities and the critical decision points within the use cases. Some use cases are

exceptionally complex and may require analysis with State Transition Diagrams (see Chapter 12).

2. *Model the domain.* The analysis model includes a class diagram representing the business entities that exist in the user's environment or domain (see Chapters 10 and 11). This model secures your fundamental understanding of the "things" that you will automate and the long-lived transactions that the system you build will need to manage.

3. *Realize the use cases.* Every use case deemed necessary for the software must exist as a set of collaborations among business entities represented in your class diagram. We use sequence diagrams to ensure that all essential business entities exist. We also ensure that the business entities possess the necessary attributes to fulfill their responsibilities and, further, that the business entities can carry out their responsibilities by working with other entities in the class diagram to meet the goals of a use case. Each use case will possess at least one sequence diagram for this purpose (see Chapter 13).

Specifying the requirements involves detailing the attributes, methods, and relationships of all the classes in the analysis model. The result of this work is the Software Requirements Specification (SRS). The SRS is the final authority on the requirements. Additionally, you may need to specify the interfaces to your system in an Interface Requirements Specification (IRS).

1. *Specify the requirements.* You analyze the user requirements represented in the use cases to understand what the system must do to fulfill those user requirements. The result of this analysis is a set of requirements, attributes, methods, and relationships, organized in a specification. Both the analysis model and the use cases exist in the SRS (see Chapter 14 for more about this extremely valuable and important concept).

2. *Specify the interface requirements.* Frequently, the system you are building must communicate with other systems. If your system communicates with other systems, someone must specify the interface between your system and each of the other systems. The Interface Requirements Specification (IRS) serves as a contract between you and your interfacing systems. As such, the IRS imposes requirements on your system. (We describe the IRS, its development, and its contents in Chapter 15.)

Verifying and validating the requirements are a two-part process. Validating the requirements involves taking steps to ensure that you have the right requirements. Verifying the requirements involves taking steps to ensure that you have the requirements right. Validation involves the user because it is the user who knows what the user wants. Verification is an engineering activity best carried out by engineers and programmers.

1. *Present storyboards of the requirements to the user.* A storyboard is a pictorial walk-through of significant instances of use cases to demonstrate to users that you understand their requirements. You need a storyboard for each use case. If the use case logic is complex, you may need more than one (see Chapter 9).

2. *Develop test cases from the SRS.* The SRS represents a control flow model of the system you are building. Rewriting this control flow model as one that is suitable for building test cases gives you valuable insight into the clarity and completeness of your specification. Not only does this activity result in a better set of requirements, it leads you to begin the test process up front (see Chapter 16).

Moving from Requirements to Design

The analysis model is an excellent start to the design model. In design, you deal with issues you have not yet dealt with in analysis. These include managing collections, managing persistent data, applying design patterns, implementing the presentation, isolating interfaces, and managing concurrency. As a result, you can expect to have three to five times the number of classes in the design model than in the analysis model.

Building the User Requirements

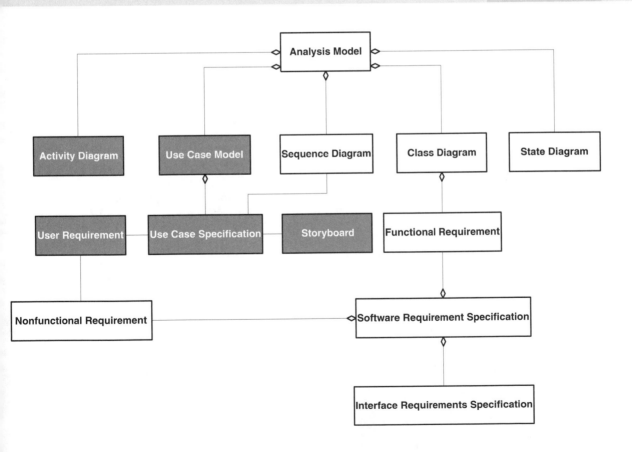

Getting to Know the Problem Domain

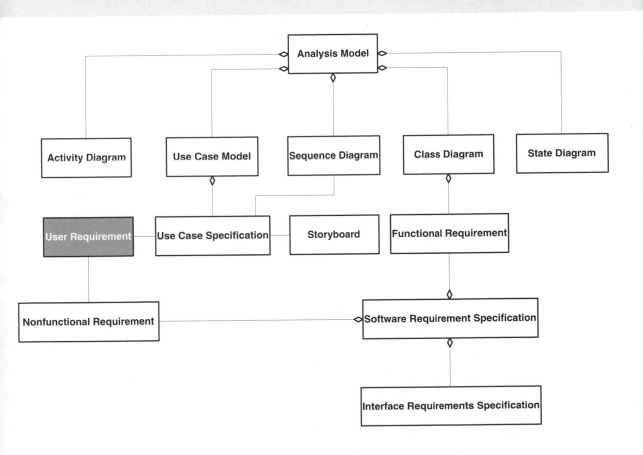

Normally, we are not experts in the fields for which our systems provide automation, so the first thing we must do is to familiarize ourselves with the area we are attempting to automate. We need to understand the processes for the given field to understand how automation facilitates those processes. This almost always requires us to become researchers. In fact, we find the biggest challenge of specifying a new system is the research that goes into learning the problem domain. A problem domain is defined as the knowledge area in which the problem is defined. Before we can get to know the problem domain, we must be able to speak the language of our user community.

Researching the Area

One of our goals for the research is to be able to speak our users' language. Each field for which we have provided an application has had its own set of terms and acronyms. Domain experts use these terms and acronyms as if these were common to the English language. Often, domain experts use the terms without realizing people outside the field do not understand what they mean. At first, our users' language seems to be jargon, but as we become more proficient, it begins to make sense to us.

It is important that we capture the knowledge we gain about the language of the problem domain. We do this in a glossary. As we run across phrases, acronyms, and unfamiliar words or words with definitions specific to the problem domain, we record them along with their definitions in our glossary. We periodically ask someone from our user community to review this document. These reviews help us ensure that we are using our users' language correctly. The glossary helps us gradually build our vocabulary in the language of the problem domain while giving us the opportunity to improve communications with our user community. Once we know the words, we next get to know the business.

A major goal of researching the problem domain is to understand the underlying business goals. If we can understand what the user is trying to accomplish, we are better prepared to understand why our users need certain processes. If we can keep in mind what the user is really trying to achieve, we can better recommend ways to achieve those goals. We also need to understand that different users see the same problem differently.

Often, people with different responsibilities see things from different perspectives. A group of people with one set of responsibilities may have a perspective very different from that of a group of people with a different set of responsibilities, even though both groups are viewing the same problem domain. For example, one user may see an application as an action request system, whereas another user may see the same application as a contracting system. These different perspectives lead each group to have different, and sometimes competing, goals and desires. It is often a difficult job to enable every group to realize its unique set of goals. If you fail to consider each group's point of view, that group will resist using the application. In fact, the application may fail entirely because you failed to consider the point of view of an important group of users. Now that we know what we wish to obtain from our research, we need to know how to get there.

Researching a new area of knowledge, or problem domain, can be a bit overwhelming. Suppose we need to develop an application to assist doctors in diagnosing a patient's illness. Would we then have to attend medical school before attempting the application? We could not afford to go to that extreme to learn about diagnosing patients' illnesses. If we did, we might produce only one or two applications in a career. So what can we do? We can narrow the scope of our problem domain.

In the example, the scope of our problem would not be all of medicine but only issues directly related to diagnosing illnesses. Without having to learn all about medicine, we would likely be able to learn much about how a doctor diagnoses a patient. We might learn that basic tests and patient-provided information give the doctor enough information to determine if a diagnosis is possible or if additional tests are necessary. We may be able to build a system that helps the doctor by providing a list of possible diagnoses. The system may also provide a list of additional tests that may confirm or refute each of the diagnoses. Clearly, we must limit the scope of our research in order to be effective.

Reading, Reading, Reading

Reading is one of the most effective research tools. A wealth of knowledge is readily available in nearly every field of interest. Reading builds your knowledge level about the subject independently of the user community. The knowledge you gain helps you follow your users' discussion of the problem domain with a higher level of understanding. Of course, with so much to read, where should one start? Introductory books on a subject and professional magazines are often a good start.

We often ask some of our customers to recommend a good introductory book on the subject. If our system is to service multiple groups, we ask a representative from each group for a recommendation. You should stay with introductory information. It is simply unrealistic in most cases to become an expert. Remember to keep the scope of the problem domain in mind. If the scope becomes too large, the amount of necessary reading also becomes too large. We also ask our customers if they subscribe to professional journals or other magazines that focus on the given domain.

Magazines often provide short, concise articles on various aspects of a problem domain. This can be an excellent way to build your level of knowledge on the subject. There may be search facilities for magazines. These are frequently available on web sites or on CD-ROM. Ask your customer if these facilities can be made available to you. You may also ask the customer to recommend articles that address his issues of concern.

Another great source of information is operating procedures or processes. Often a customer has operating procedures for a given area of the problem domain. Operating procedures tell the reader how to perform a given process to achieve the desired results. If operating procedures exist, you will definitely want to read through them. Checklists might also be available for some of the tasks that must be performed. These, too, are important tools for teaching the problem domain. Related software systems may already be built in the same domain as the one your customer is requesting.

If a current software system exists, study that system as a source of information. If you are replacing another automated system, you can extract valuable information from that system. Find out what functions the current system provides and for whom it provides each function. Ask users what they find effective about the current system. Conversely, discover what the users consider to be the shortcomings of the current system. Of course, the number one source of information is the users themselves.

Interviewing the Customer and Users

Customers and users are the best source of information about the problem domain that you will need to address. A major challenge to interviewing the users and customers is that they never have enough time to give you. We often hear and have read about joint development between the users and the developers. In joint development, a user works full time with the analysis team. This seems to us to be a wonderful process that will help analysis significantly. If this arrangement were possible, we would definitely choose to work this way. Joint development allows the user to watch each step as you gather and analyze requirements. This helps both you and the user catch and correct any misconceptions and incorrect assumptions right away.

Unfortunately, we have never been given this opportunity. Our users' available time for the project has always been somewhat limited, so we must make effective use of the time we can get from users. We need to be prepared to make effective use of our users' time when we speak to them, and we need to ensure that we accurately and completely capture the information they provide us.

To do this effectively, we must decide how we will meet with them. We could choose to have structured meetings with a large group of users representing each distinct category of user. We might also choose to have separate meetings with each group of users from the same category. We might also meet with very small groups or individuals to discuss the system. Our experience tells us to use very small groups or even individuals in the early stages of requirements gathering when we are trying to determine vision and scope of the system. We may use the same groups to determine the completeness of our list of use cases (see Chapter 5). We might choose larger groups from a given category of users to storyboard our understanding of the requirements (see Chapter 9). Table 4.1 lists the core set of meetings you should conduct; realize that you might need to conduct each meeting more than once.

We prepare for these meetings so that we get the most out of them. We always walk into the interview with a list of questions. Some of these questions come from gaps in our research, but many others are canned questions

TABLE 4.1
Core Meetings

Artifact	When	Who
Vision and Scope	At start of project	A representative from each user group
Use Case Names and Descriptions	After initial research	A representative from each user group
Storyboards	After use case specification	Several representatives from each user group

TABLE 4.2
Sample Open-Ended Questions

What are the most important aspects of the problem domain you would like the application to address?
What parts of the problem domain are often overlooked and end up causing problems?
What do you believe the application must do to be effective?
How are the processes completed now?
How do you expect a new system to make you more effective?
Are there any inherent limitations in the way you do business that might affect the new system?

designed to extract needed information. Certain questions are always good to ask. Table 4.2 lists a few we consistently use.

These are but a few examples. A common thread runs through all these questions: they are all open-ended. Open-ended questions prompt users and customers to talk about the problem domain.

We are trying to learn about the problem domain and the users' expectations. We should be ready to listen intently. We should keep the users and customers talking about the problem domain. Because we keep our questions as open-ended as possible, users often take the conversations in directions we did not think of. This leads to the kind of information we might have otherwise overlooked. We also try to involve these same users in the storyboarding efforts later to verify that we have captured their points of view accurately.

Now that we have all this information, what do we do with it?

Building the Use Cases

In addition to the glossary we discussed earlier, we start building our domain model when we begin our research. The domain model captures the entities and events associated with the area we are studying. We always use a class diagram (see Chapter 11) to capture the problem domain in a domain model. We deem it important to store information about what we are learning as soon as possible lest we forget it. The analysis model, especially the class diagram, is a great tool for storing this knowledge. Although we discuss use cases first, they are built in parallel to other artifacts in the analysis model.

An important artifact to help us capture the knowledge we have gained is a use case. Use cases view the system one function or service at a time. To write use cases, we pick a function the system performs for the customers or users and examine that function step by step until the function is complete. As we discuss next, we can isolate most use cases by first identifying the users and interfaces of the system. We then identify the functions or services the system provides for the user, group of users, or interfaces. And so we come to our next topic, use cases.

Actors and Use Cases

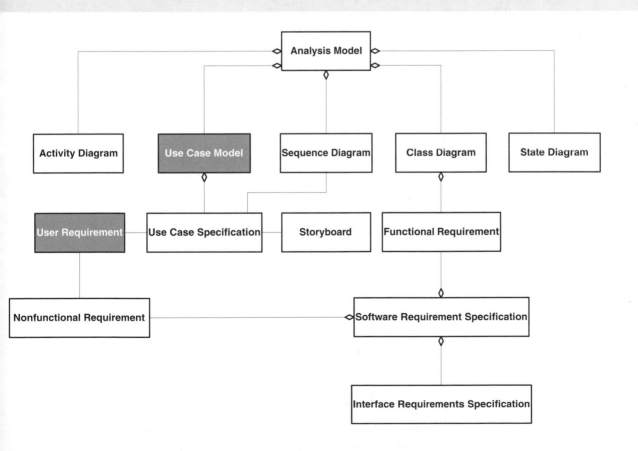

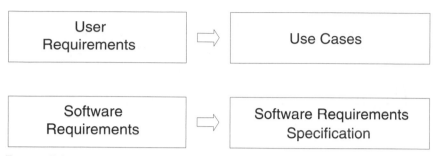

FIGURE 5.1
User and software requirements

A use case is a description of the usage of a system from one or more users' point of view. The usage accomplishes some action of value for some user. The value the use case provides may not be to the user triggering the use case. The user can be a person, another system, or even an internal system entity such as a timer. We use the term actor because it is a more generic term that does not imply a human user.

A use case describes the interaction between the actor and the system. The analyst specifies the use case by completing a standard collection of information. The collection includes the following:

- Description of the use case
- State of the system at the start of the use case
- State of the system at the end of the use case
- Normal sequence of events describing the interaction between the actor and the system
- Any alternative courses to the normal sequence of events
- Any system reactions to exceptions the system encounters

The set of use cases describes the user requirements for the system. This set is the functionality representing everything the user wants the system to accomplish. We derive the software requirements from the use cases during analysis. The software requirements consist of all the requirements the software must demonstrate for the system to meet the user requirements. Figure 5.1 illustrates these levels of requirements.

Occasionally, the software requirements and the use cases overlap. However, the software requirements represent the developer's point of view. The use cases represent the user's point of view. Your goal when writing the use cases is to communicate the user requirements as clearly as possible, using the language of the user. In this chapter, we describe how to discover the use cases and actors for a system by first defining the boundaries of the system and then finding the system's actors and use cases.

Defining the Boundaries of the System _____

In this process, we use context diagramming to understand the system boundaries. Context diagramming is a technique in which you seek to understand the environment within which this system will operate by defining all interactions between your system and the entities in the environment. The result is a list of entities the system interacts with and a description of the nature of the interactions.

You begin the context diagram by representing the system you are specifying as a single circle. You then list the users and systems that interact with your system. Understanding the nature of the interactions identifies potential actors to your system. Table 5.1 provides a starting point for finding actors and their interactions.

TABLE 5.1
Potential Change Management Actors

Potential Actors	Questions to Ask Yourself
Human Users	Who needs information from the system?
	What information do they get?
	Does the system provide it on-demand, periodically, or both?
	Who provides information to the system?
	What information do they provide?
	Is the system required to respond?
Other Systems	Which systems can cause your system to react?
	Does your system have an option, or must it respond?
	Is the request periodic, or is it unpredictable?
	Which system must respond to a request from your system?
	Does your system send the request periodically?

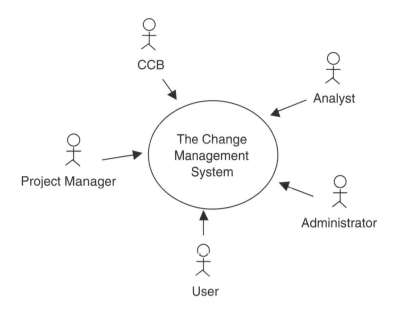

FIGURE 5.2
Change management context

Consider a system that manages change requests and defect reports for one or more systems. Project managers use the system to manage change requests associated with their projects. Change Control Boards (CCB) use the system to manage change requests and approve the releases in which the change requests are implemented. Analysts use the system to update status information as they analyze change requests. Administrators manage user and system information. Finally, general users with appropriate access use the Change Management System to view the status of change requests and releases. Figure 5.2 illustrates an example context diagram for this Change Management System.

Once you have identified the users and the systems that interact with your system, you can begin to identify and define the actors to your system. When you review the list of users, you will realize that some users really impose similar demands on the system. Therefore, an actor can represent one or more users.

Begin by defining the nature of the interaction. At this point, your description should be a goal-oriented description. For example, a potential actor for a change management system is the project manager. The following text is an example description for this actor.

Actor: *Project Manager*

Description: *The Project Manager uses the system to produce a report that lists all releases of all systems affected by a particular change request.*

While this is a solid potential use case, it is just one of many potential use cases for this actor. A better way to describe the actor is to use a goal-oriented description that doesn't limit the potential use cases. The following is an example of a goal-oriented description for this actor:

Actor: *Project Manager*

Description: *The Project Manager uses the application to manage change requests and associate the change request with one or more versions of a system.*

The second description does not limit the project manager's use of the system. Many potential use cases support the goal embodied in the second description. You will find those use cases in later work.

Table 5.2 presents a list of actors for the Change Management System.

TABLE 5.2
Change Management Actors

Actor	Description
Project Manager	The project manager uses the application to manage change requests and associate the change request with one or more versions of a system.
Administrator	The administrator uses the application to add and maintain user and system information.
Analyst	The analyst uses the application to reflect the status of change requests as work on the change request progresses.
Change Control Board	The CCB uses the application to approve change requests for inclusion in a version and to approve a version for release into production.
User	A user uses the application to submit work requests.

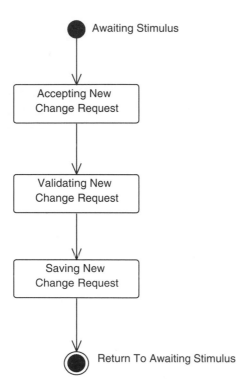

Awaiting Stimulus

Accepting New
Change Request

Validating New
Change Request

Saving New
Change Request

Return To Awaiting Stimulus

FIGURE 5.3
Use case states

Moving from Steady State to Steady State _____

Use cases are best bounded by steady state to steady state. A use case begins in a steady state, receives an input or stimulus, responds to the actor, transitions through one or more intermediate states, and finally transitions to the final steady state, as shown in Figure 5.3. Any transition can result in the use case providing an output.

A steady state is a condition of the system such that the system is ready to respond to any of a number of stimuli leading to any of a number of use cases. This differs from an intermediate state in that in an intermediate state, the system is expecting one of a limited set of stimuli in order to complete the use case. For example, if the use case is to enter a new change request, the system starts in the steady state. The system at this point can accept a new change request and provide information on existing change requests or any of a number of other user actions. Once the user has requested a new change request and the system is providing the opportunity for the user to type the change request information, the system enters an intermediate state. At this point, the system is in an "Accepting New Change Request" state. The user can do one of two things: provide the change request information or, perhaps, cancel the request. Once the user provides the information, the system may enter a "Validating New Change Request" state. Once the system validates the new change request, the system enters the "Saving New Change Request" state. When the system finishes saving the change request, the system acknowledges the creation of the new change request to the user and enters the final steady state.

At times, you may write a use case that crosses steady states. This rare occurrence results because your goal in writing use cases is simplicity. For example, your system may send a message to another system as part of a use case. Once the message is sent, the system is in a steady state. However, to simplify the use case, you may include processing any reject messages from the external system in this use case. It is obvious to the casual observer that the use case has crossed a steady state. However, the simplicity of this approach better serves the reader.

Identifying Use Cases

Next, you identify all the use cases that the system must implement to meet the needs of the actors. This process involves examining each actor with the purpose of identifying each interaction. It also involves examining internal events that may trigger a system action.

For each user, you should identify each discrete use of the system. In the classic Automated Teller Machine (ATM) example, we can identify the methods in which a customer might interact with the system by asking what the system does for the user. The user may check an account balance, withdraw cash, deposit funds, and transfer funds from one account to another. These are all examples of use cases for the ATM system. Additionally, one more use case comes to mind. The ATM system always authenticates the user before any of these uses are allowed.

There are a number of examples from the change management system. The user may enter a new request for a change to a system, assign change requests to a version release of a system, and approve a version for release to production. You will be able to identify many of these use cases from your research and by understanding the questions in Table 5.1. You will find more use cases through interviews and meetings with your user.

Next, examine all incoming and outgoing messages for each system that interacts with your system. Many of the incoming messages represent use cases. Although outgoing messages do not represent use cases, they can assure you that you did not miss an event that caused your system to send the message.

Finally, you should examine periodic and timed events to determine if they would generate a use case. For example, your system may be required to perform a certain activity at the same time every day. Another situation in which a use case could be appropriate is upon the expiration of a timer. For example, your system may be required to send a message interrogating an interfacing system for input if your system has not received any input from the interfacing system in the last five minutes.

Introducing the Change Management System Example

We used the example of a Change Management System to discuss context diagrams and discovery of actors and use cases. In Sidebar 5.1 we formalize the description of a Change Management System. We use this example throughout the remaining chapters as a common frame of reference.

We identified all the actors for our Change Management System in Defining the Boundaries of the System in this chapter. Table 5.3 lists the use cases we identified in our research and the system introduction above.

SIDEBAR 5.1
FORMAL DESCRIPTION OF A CHANGE MANAGEMENT SYSTEM

In the building of a Problem Reporting/Change Management System, a few terms must be defined and a few concepts must be stated.

A system is any collection of hardware and/or software components that provides service to the user. A system can consist of any number of hardware and/or software components. Each of these components can itself be a system.

Four types of Problems/Change Request are at issue: Work Orders, Change Requests, Software Defect Reports, and Request for New Systems. The last three types of change requests are directly related to software and are referred to from this point on as Change Orders.

A Work Report is worked individually throughout its life cycle until resolved and verified complete.

A Change Order is worked individually only to a certain point in its life cycle. It is then assigned to a release or version of a given software system.

Software is released to the user community in versions. A version or release of a software system includes one or more Change Orders.

A version or release of the software is normally worked as a project. Some Change Orders can require multiple software systems to change. This is often referred to as a Program. In our context, a program is a project with multiple subprojects. A Change Order that represents a program will have one or more subordinate change requests so that each software system that requires work has a Change Order. Once a Change Order is assigned to a version, the status of the Change Order is the same as that of the version.

When an incident happens to a user, the user may not be sure if it represents a Work Order or Change Order. The system allows the user to enter whatever request the user thinks is appropriate. The analyst or project manager may change the type of a request into another type of request.

When the user is initiating a request, it may not be clear which system or subsystem is truly at issue. The system allows the user to assign the request to whatever system the user thinks is appropriate. The analyst or project manager may reassign the request to a different system or subsystem.

TABLE 5.3
Change Management Use Case List

Use Case Name	Brief Description
Add User	An administrator adds a user to the system by providing identification information and assigning one or more roles.
Edit User	An administrator changes user information.
Delete User	An administrator deletes an existing user.
Add System	An administrator adds a system by providing identification information.
Edit System	An administrator changes system information.
Delete System	An administrator deletes a system.
Draft Work Request	A user drafts a work request for a system.
View/Edit Change Order	A user views or edits information about a change order.
View/Edit Work Order	A user views or edits information about a work order.
Manage Change Order	A user changes the status of a change order.
Create Version	A user creates a version for a system.
View/Edit Version	A user views or edits version information.
Assign Change To Version	A user assigns a change order to a version.
Remove Change From Version	A user removes a change order from a version.
Approve a Version for Work	A user approves a given version to allow work to begin.
Approve a Version for Release	A user approves a version for release into production.

Modeling Use Cases

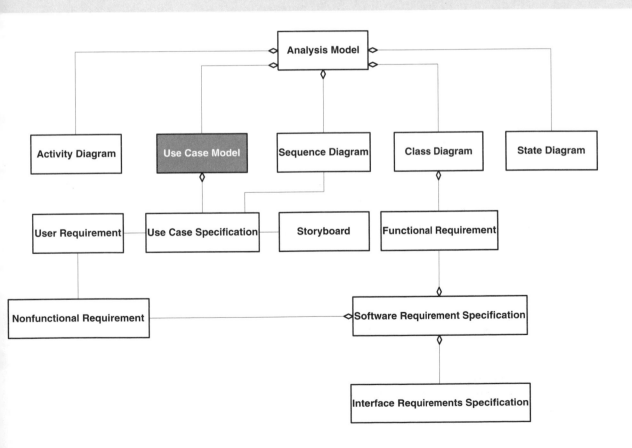

An Actor   A Use Case

FIGURE 6.1
Use case notation

Once you have identified the use cases, you can begin modeling them. The Unified Modeling Language (UML) defines a standard notation for diagramming use cases. Once you have a first draft of the use case model, you will find common behavior that leads to generalizing use cases. You can then show the dependencies between use cases. The dependency can be an INCLUDES relationship or an EXTENDS relationship. Finally, we discuss how to package the use cases into groups of related use cases. This packaging helps with the manageability of the use case model.

Diagramming Use Cases

The UML uses ovals to represent use cases with the name listed directly below the oval. The UML uses stick figures to represent actors. You represent the relationship between an actor and a use case with a line between the two. This relationship can be a one-way or two-way flow of information. An arrow points away from the initiator of the action. Figure 6.1 illustrates this notation.

An actor can interact with more than one use case. In this instance, the actor can initiate or receive results from more than one service of the system you are specifying. Similarly, a use case can interact with more than one actor. In this instance, the use case is providing the same service to more than one actor. For example, a clerk at a mail order catalog company may enter an order on your behalf in accordance with a phone conversation. Alternatively, a wholesale purchaser may send an order to the company electronically. Both actors, the clerk and the customer order system, are interacting with the use case "Enter Order." This example is illustrated in Figure 6.2.

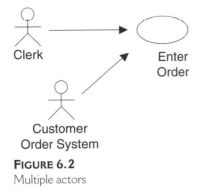

FIGURE 6.2
Multiple actors

Generalizing Use Cases

Use cases contain system actions. At times, these actions repeat within several use cases. You should keep an eye out for instances of repeating actions within multiple use cases, with the goal of extracting common behavior. You can then use the extracted behavior across all the use cases that exhibit this common behavior.

Generalization, in this sense, is the modularization of use cases. The benefits you gain from modularization include simplified maintenance, consistency, and reuse. Maintenance of the system requires you to update the use cases. You need to update common functionality spread across several use cases. When you generalize this common functionality, you can update it in one place. This activity also bestows the benefit of consistency. You can minimize the effort you spend ensuring that all validation, for example, responds consistently across all use cases. Reusing common functionality also saves development effort. You can simply invoke the use case that provides the common behavior instead of rewriting a new use case.

The challenge you face with generalization is to minimize the complexity you introduce when the reader must link several use cases together to understand the real use case, sometimes referred to as the "concrete" use case, the actor sees. The real use case is the combined behavior of the primary use case and any generalized use cases. If the user needs to link too many use cases together to understand the functionality, you defeat the purpose of the use cases by making it harder for the user to confirm that you understand his needs.

Generalizing Use Cases for the Change Management System

In the Change Management System, every use case requires the user to authenticate before executing the purpose of the use case. This requirement ensures that the system knows which use cases the user is authorized to execute and the systems to which the user has access. Instead of rewriting this common behavior in each of the use cases, we simply generalize the authentication process into the login use case.

Relationships Among Use Cases

Use cases may relate to each other in one of two ways: INCLUDES and EXTENDS. These two relationships can result because one use case requires another real use case in order to be real or because a use case requires a generalized use case to be real. The INCLUDES relationship specifies that one use case is included in another use case. The included use case is required to complete the behavior necessary for the including use case to accomplish its work. The including use case has no option to perform or not perform the sequence of actions specified in the included use case—performance is a must.

The EXTENDS relationship specifies that the use case extends another use case. The EXTENDS use case may be required by the extending use case to accomplish its goal. The EXTENDS relationship differs from the INCLUDES relationship in that the EXTENDS relationship is conditional. When you specify the extending use case, you must specify the conditions under which you will include the additional sequence of actions in the use case you are specifying. Figure 6.3 illustrates the notation for these two relationships.

Diagramming Change Management System Use Cases

The change management system implements 17 use cases. We have specified the roles of the users into five actors. Figure 6.4 represents a subset of

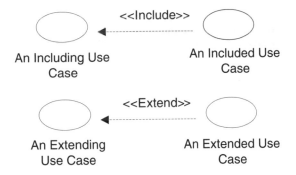

FIGURE 6.3
INCLUDES and EXTENDS

the use cases for the change management system. You can study the full use case model in Appendix B.

An actor named the user might *DRAFT A WORK REQUEST*. Remember that the actor describes a role, not an individual. A number of individuals can fulfill the role described by the actor. The analyst might *VIEW OR EDIT A WORK ORDER, VIEW OR EDIT A CHANGE ORDER,* or *MANAGE A CHANGE ORDER.* The

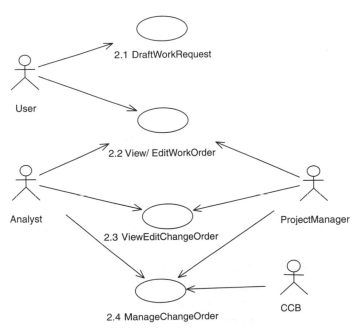

FIGURE 6.4
Change Management use case

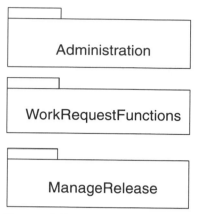

FIGURE 6.5
Change Management use case packages

Project Manager might perform the same functions, using the Change Management System. The Change Control Board (CCB) might *MANAGE A CHANGE ORDER.*

Packaging Use Cases

Most systems you specify will require you to group use cases into packages. Grouping like use cases into a single package helps organize the use cases, eases the search for functionality, and provides an organized presentation. During analysis you will frequently need to revisit specific use cases to refresh your memory about specific functionality. The packages you choose will help find the appropriate use cases quickly. Figure 6.5 shows the packages for the Change Management System.

Packaging the Change Management System Use Cases

We have packaged the 17 use cases for the change management into three packages. The first package includes all the use cases related to administering the Change Management System. The second package includes all the use cases related to managing work request. The third package includes all the use cases related to managing a release of a system. Table 6.1 identifies the packages and their contents.

TABLE 6.1
Change Management Use Case Packages

Package Name	Use Cases
Administrative Functions	Login
	Add User
	Edit User
	Delete User
	Add System
	Edit System
	Delete System
Work Request Functions	Draft Work Request
	View/Edit Change Order
	View/Edit Work Order
	Manage Change Order
Manage Release	Create Version
	View/Edit Version
	Assign Change to Version
	Remove Change from Version
	Approve Version for work
	Approve Version for Release

Using Activity Diagrams to Represent Use Cases

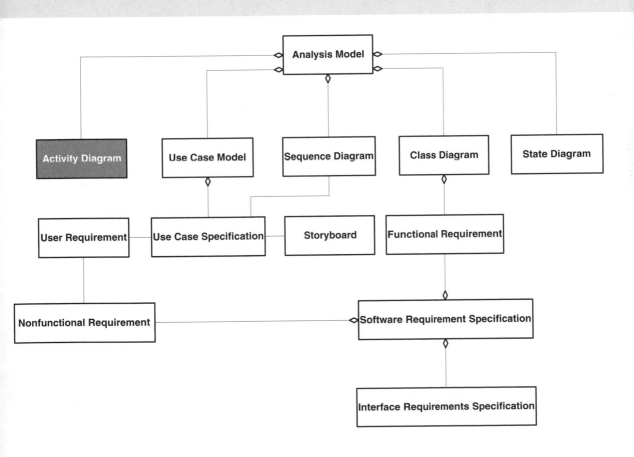

An activity diagram is a type of flow chart. We use activity diagrams to visually model the dynamic behavior of a given part of our system. Flow charts have been around for quite a while. It seems that most software modeling methodologies use the flow chart in one form or another. Although many people associate flow charts with older modeling methods, flow charts are still an effective tool for modeling today.

Activity diagrams can be used to model the dynamic behavior of a number of elements of an object-oriented system. One element that activity diagrams can be very effective in modeling is the behavior of an operation on a class. The specifics of a class are discussed in a later chapter, but it is enough to know now that an operation represents some service a class provides to the system. We could show the dynamic behavior of a given operation by using an activity diagram. Another use of the activity diagram is to model use cases. We concentrate on use cases later in this chapter. First, we need to understand the elements of the activity diagram so that we can build them.

Elements of Activity Diagrams

The activity diagram consists of five elements: Activity, Transition, Decision, Synchronization Bars, and Swim Lanes. It is not necessary that each activity diagram contain each element. In fact, we could have many activity diagrams with only Activities and Transitions. These five elements used together give us enough tools to use activity diagrams effectively.

Activities represent a task that must be performed and are, therefore, the basic building block of an Activity Diagram. Activities appear in our model as rectangles with rounded corners. Activities are normally given names that begin with a verb followed by the object being acted upon. For example, an Activity could be named "Display Screen," as is the case in Figure 7.1. How do you know what task should appear on an Activity? Determining the answer is largely situational. You must decide to what depth to break down the activity so that the reader can gain a complete understanding without being overburdened with details.

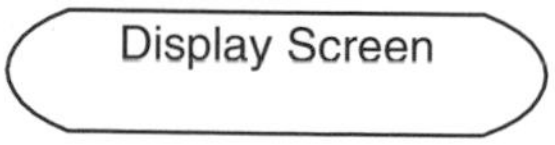

FIGURE 7.1
Notation for Activity element

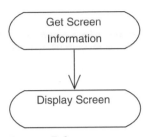

FIGURE 7.2
Transition element

When modeling use cases, we make the Activities on the Activity Diagram distinct tasks that the user would recognize. For example, we would not place the task "Initialize Count Variable" on an Activity Diagram. The user would not recognize "Initialize Count Variable" as a distinct task because it is a task the software performs. The user task could be "Print Employee Paychecks."

The Transition represents the movement from one element in the activity diagram to another and therefore shows the flow between elements. Transitions can include a good deal of information about when the Transition may occur; this information can include Events and Guard Conditions. Events describe the trigger that causes the transition. Guard Conditions ensure that the state of the system is appropriate for the transition. These are the same Transitions used in State Transition diagrams, discussed in Chapter 12. When we use activity diagrams to model use cases, we assume the appropriate System State. The majority of the time, completion of the previous activity transitions the system to the next activity, as illustrated in Figure 7.2. We do not often use Events and Guard Conditions in our activity diagrams.

In nearly every workflow or process, it is necessary to ask questions and direct the task in different directions according to the answer. This redirection, called a branch in the flow of control, allows alternative paths through the workflow. In Activity Diagrams, we reflect flow of control as a diamond shape. When modeling use cases with Activity Diagrams, we normally reflect the question on the decision point or diamond and the possible answers on the transition arrow. We also name the decision point in a form that represents a question. For example, "Count less than 10" or "Process Complete" are both taken to be questions whenever used on the label for a decision point. The example in Figure 7.3 shows a simple decision point with two possible outcomes.

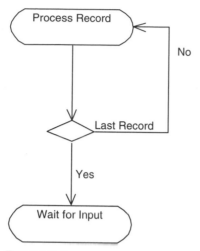

FIGURE 7.3
Decision element

The example in Figure 7.3 shows the activity of processing a record. We then ask the question, "Was that the last record?" If the answer is no, we process another record. Otherwise, we wait for additional input. This example illustrates how branching logic is normally applied.

Tasks in an Activity Diagram can occur concurrently. We can reflect this behavior by using Synchronization Bars. A fork occurs when multiple tasks begin at the completion of a single task. A join occurs when a single task cannot begin until the completion of multiple tasks that are running in parallel. The Synchronization Bar at the join ensures that tasks have provided the appropriate information and that the system is in the appropriate state for the start of the next task. Figure 7.4 shows an example of a Synchronization Bar for a fork and then a join with the same group of tasks. Allowing task to fork and join in use case modeling can help us understand dependencies in our use case.

It is often helpful to show multiple entities taking part in a given workflow. When modeling use cases, we might want to show how each actor participates in a given workflow. We accomplish this with Swim Lanes. Swim Lanes partition the activity diagram vertically. Each Swim Lane must be given a unique name. Activities are then placed in the Swim Lane of the entity that accomplishes activity. The example in Figure 7.5 shows how the actor named "user" logs in to our system.

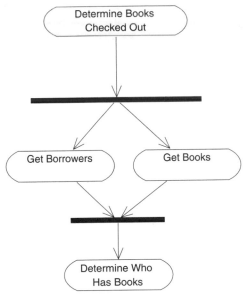

FIGURE 7.4
Synchronization Bars element for concurrent task

Figure 7.5 starts with an element that appears as a solid dot. This dot is an activity that signifies the start of the flow. The start activity may or may not include a name. We then have a transition to the activity Initialize Application. Notice that our dot is in the User Swim Lane, and the transition takes us to the Mainframe Swim Lane. The transition across the Swim Lanes User and Mainframe from the start dot to the activity Initialize Application signifies that the user must take some action to start the flow. Once the application has completed the initialization, the system transitions to the second task.

The transition from Initialize Application to Present Login Screen requires no decisions or actions. Once Initialize Application is complete, the next task simply begins. These types of activities with simple transitions are useful for breaking down a complex task into simpler tasks. It also helps ensure that no task is overlooked.

Next, the activity diagram shows the transition from Present Login Screen to Enter User Data. The system presents the login screen and then waits for user input. We represent the task for the user to enter data as an activity. Once the user completes the task, the system receives the input. The system then must determine if the user is authorized to use the system. We model the question and the resulting branches with our Decision point.

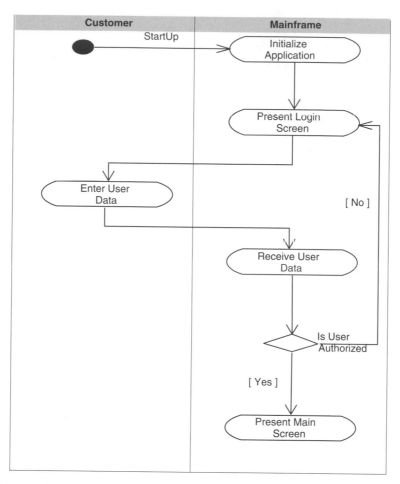

FIGURE 7.5
Swim Lanes element

The Decision point asks, "Is the user authorized?" If the answer is no, the system prompts the user to reenter the information. If the answer is yes, the system presents the main screen to the user. This is the end of this Activity Diagram. If we were modeling a system, we might refer to this Activity Diagram from a number of other activities. This would require us to model this activity only once and we could simply refer to it when we want the system to perform some other action. Let us look at an example to help understand this.

A bank ATM is a classic example. The bank ATM empowers customers to perform a number of activities on their accounts. We model transferring funds from one account to another to get a better feel for activity diagrams. To transfer funds, the ATM requires the customer to authenticate authorization to complete the activity. Having the appropriate bank card and knowing the Personal Identification Number, or PIN, accomplishes the authentication. We break the action into two parts: authentication and transfer of funds.

Breaking this sequence down into parts is helpful for two reasons. First, it keeps our activity diagrams understandable. Second, we need authentication for any transaction. By segregating a transaction into its own activity we can simply refer to it. We first look at the authentication Activity Diagram and then at an Activity Diagram for transferring money from one account to another.

Figure 7.6 shows the authentication for our ATM customer. We have two Swim Lanes, one for the customer and one for the ATM. This Activity Diagram affords the opportunity to study the authentication process in an abstract way. The abstraction allows us to concentrate on the process and not on the details.

When we study the abstraction of the authentication process, we might identify a number of questions. For example, how does the customer abandon this activity? How many opportunities should the customer be given to reenter the PIN? These are the kinds of questions that make the activity diagrams a valuable tool in analysis. The questions help us know the behavior our customer expects from the system. We will not answer these questions here but will instead look at the transfer process.

The Activity Diagram in Figure 7.7 models the way by which the bank customer transfers funds from one account to another. We added an additional Swim Lane in the Activity Diagram. Normally, a bank has a central computer system, named Mainframe in our example. The ATMs are considered clients of the mainframe. Now we must coordinate this activity through three separate entities.

This Activity Diagram illustrates the process for transferring funds from one account to another. We prompt to determine the amount of money to transfer, the losing account number, and the gaining account number. We performed all the prompting and all the data entry in only two activities. Clearly, we could use multiple activities to accomplish this activity. We could have easily prompted for the amount to transfer and waited for the input. We would then prompt for the account to transfer from and would check the amount available in the account. If it is insufficient to complete the

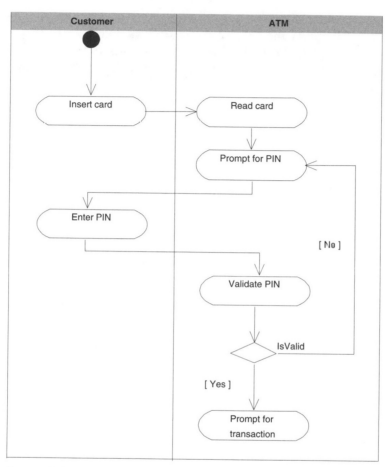

FIGURE 7.6
ATM authentication

activity, we would inform the customer; otherwise, we would prompt for the account to transfer funds to. Which way is more correct?

In this case, the customer for whom you are building the system should let you know how the system should behave. You could offer the customer several alternative system behaviors to inform the customer that choices can be made. This approach helps ensure customer satisfaction with the system by delivering a system that behaves as the customer expects.

Next, we look at an Activity Diagram from the Change Management System.

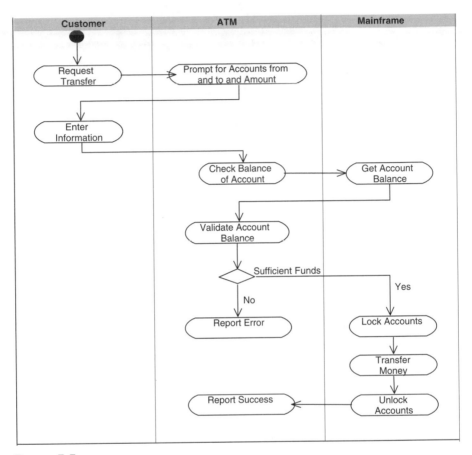

FIGURE 7.7
Funds transfer

Change Management System Activity Diagram _____

The diagram in Figure 7.8 illustrates how the user might add a change request to a version of a system. First, the user indicates the intent to add a change request to a version. The Change Management System presents a list of all available versions for the particular system. The user selects a version to work with. The Change Management System presents the version information along with all unassigned, opened change requests associated with

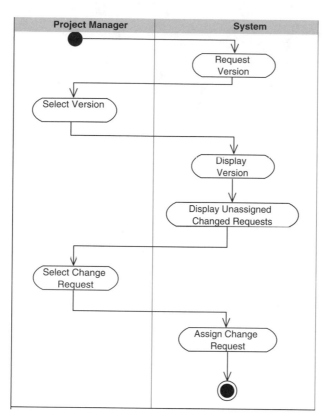

FIGURE 7.8
Assign change request to version

the selected system. The user selects a change request from the list for inclusion in the version. The Change Management System assigns the change request to the selected version.

Writing Use Cases

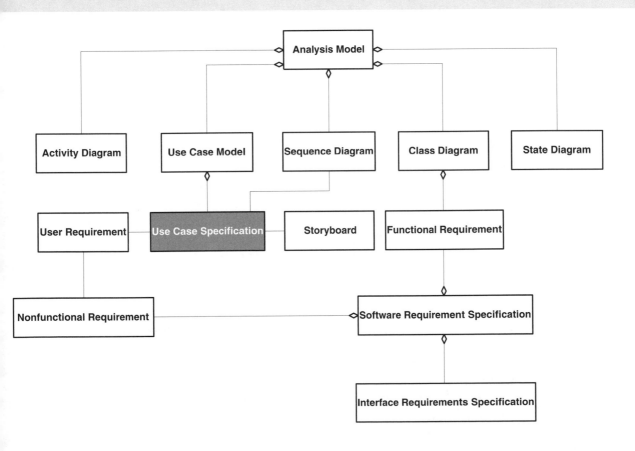

Writing use cases is the specification of the user requirements. This work solidifies much of the knowledge you have gained up to this point in the process. Writing use cases includes understanding how to specify preconditions and postconditions. We discuss how to write preconditions, postconditions, the normal course of events, alternative courses, and exceptions. We also discuss how to determine whether you should specify an alternative course or a separate use case. This chapter introduces the use of a template for writing use cases. In addition, this chapter discusses conventions for the specifications. Finally, the chapter introduces a use case from the Change Management System.

Template Use

Use cases come in many forms. Almost every book or paper you read will describe a different format for your use cases. Along with differing formats, you will find three basic approaches for writing use cases, with many variations on these basic approaches. The first approach is to write a use case specification for each use case. The second approach is to combine similar events into a single business event and then write a use case at the higher-level business event. This approach then requires a use case scenario for each significantly different interaction below the business event. For example, in an earlier chapter we discussed a customer service representative entering an order and a wholesaler entering an order through an automated system. The second approach requires a use case named ENTER ORDER and two scenarios, one named ENTER ORDER BY CUSTOMER REP and a second scenario named RECEIVE ORDER FROM WHOLESALER. The third approach is to tailor the amount of information you provide in the use cases on the basis of the risk the use case presents to the project. In this approach, you simply provide a short description of some use cases while "fully dressing" other use cases with preconditions, postconditions, a normal course of events, and all other elements considered part of the use case.

Our approach involves writing a use case specification for each use case. This allows you to quickly find what the system is to do while ensuring that an appropriate level of understanding can be communicated to all project members. Given this, using a template provides a framework from which to approach writing the use case. The template not only ensures that you include, or at least consider, all the necessary information, it also ensures that your use cases are in the same format. A common format makes reading the use cases easier. A common format also makes it feasible to import the use cases into a requirements management tool.

The basic template for a use case includes a section for all the necessary parts. Table 8.1 lists all the elements of the use case template. The table also indicates whether the element is optional or mandatory and the phase of the requirements process in which you should complete the element.

TABLE 8.1
Elements of a Use Case

Mandatory	Element	Phase
✔	Author and date of the first version	Gathering
	Author and date of the latest revision	Throughout
✔	Actors	Gathering
✔	Use case description	Gathering
✔	Preconditions	Specification
✔	Postconditions	Specification
	Priority	Gathering
✔	Normal course of events	Specification
	Alternate courses	Specification
✔	Exceptions	Specification
	Includes	Gathering
	Notes	Throughout

Step-by-Step Description

Our use case template has 11 parts, not all of which are required. Also, not all parts are provided on the initial development of the use cases. Three passes through the use cases typically result in the information required for the entire template. The first pass results in the use case survey. The second pass results in the use case draft. The third pass results in the generalized use cases.

During development of the use case survey, the author provides the use case identifier, the author name and date information, the list of actors, and the use case description. The use case identifier consists of a project unique identifier and the use case name. We recommend that you number the use cases sequentially within the packages you identified earlier. The author and date information may seem insignificant, but this information can be critical. You should always identify the author(s) and the date the use case was first created. Similarly, you should always identify the author(s) who made the latest modification to the use case and the date the latest use case modification was made. Remember that the requirements development process is iterative. You will revisit use cases several times during development of the requirements. Nothing will aggravate you more than not understanding who changed a particular use case and when. Identifying the author and date lets you associate use case revisions with significant rewrites resulting from defect corrections or from reviews with the users. If you know the date of the defect corrections or reviews, you can determine whether you changed the use cases as a result of those reviews.

During development of the use case draft, you will add the preconditions, the postconditions, the normal course of events, any alternative courses, and exceptions. We discuss alternative courses and exceptions in the following sections. For now, we focus on preconditions, postconditions, and the normal course of events.

Preconditions represent the state of the system when the use case begins. They are a promise from the developer of the system to the user. The developer of the system is saying that if these conditions hold true, I will provide the specified results. The system developer will think of preconditions as values of system attributes. For example, in the Change Management System, we have a use case to "Edit a Work Request." This use case requires, as a precondition, that the work request exist. If the work request does not exist, you are not in this use case and the system developer cannot promise any results. A common error when writing preconditions is to include receipt of messages or user input as a precondition. Message receipt and user input are included, probably as the first step, in the normal course of events. They do not represent preconditions since they are transient events and do not represent system state information.

Postconditions include only changes to the state of the system. For example, adding a new work request changes the state of the system because a new record now exists. Sending the new work request to an external system does not affect the state of the system because the state of the system does not change as a result of the output. Transient outputs belong only in the normal course of events. Both preconditions and postconditions are written in terms of the state of the system. For example, if the use case were to allow the user to enter a new work request, the postcondition might be stated as follows:

Postcondition: *The new work request exists.*

The normal course of events describes the interaction between the user and the system. The normal course can include sequential steps, conditional logic, and iteration. Sequential steps are exactly what they sound like. The actor performs one or more actions. The system performs one or more actions in response to that stimulus. The steps follow in sequence between the system and the actor until the use case achieves its goal. The wording is informal and conversational. For example:

The user indicates the intent to submit a new change request.

The system prompts for the change request name, project name, and change request description from the user.

Conditional logic enables you to specify different system reactions on the basis of existing conditions. You use structured English to specify conditional logic. This includes the IF statement and a standard set of Boolean expressions. The IF statement lets you compare one or more conditions and then act according to the results of the evaluation. For example, suppose your system takes an action based on one of two possible user responses. The conditional statement for this would look like:

If the user responds with A, the system performs X. Otherwise, the system performs Y.

At times you will find that the user may respond with more than two choices. In this situation, you must specify nested conditions. The IF statement would be phrased as follows:

If the user responded A, the system performs X. Otherwise, if the user responded B, the system performs Y. Otherwise, the system performs Z.

Notice the conversational style. You write use cases in the language of the user to communicate clearly with the user while maintaining clear, correct, and unambiguous meaning in your use cases. You may be tempted to introduce a more formal version of structured English into the use case specification. Yield to the temptation only if you can find a balance such that you do not compromise your goal of communicating with the user.

In addition to nested conditions, you will occasionally need compound conditions. In this case, the condition you are evaluating is based on more than one test. We introduce Boolean operators into the use case specification for this purpose. For example, suppose you have to test two conditions before deciding on a system action. The first condition depends on a user response. The second condition depends on a system state value. The IF statement would look like this:

If the user responded A and the system state is B, the system performs Z.

The Boolean operators, in precedence, are AND, OR, and IS. In a few cases, you may need to use parentheses to ensure that the Boolean operators evaluate in the order you expect.

Alternative Courses

An alternative course is a sequence of actions that accomplishes the same purpose as a primary sequence of actions. Conditional statements represent branches in sequences of action the system takes to accomplish a use case. At times, you will find it useful to include both sequences of action in the normal course of events. There are times, however, when you will need to pick one of the sequences of action to place into an alternative course to simplify the reading of the use case.

Two primary situations result in possible alternative courses.

The first is a condition that requires you to separate sequences of action based on input, the state of the system, or both. Both separate courses normally join to set the system state and perhaps produce an output. Figure 8.1 illustrates this situation.

In this case, you have two choices. The first choice is to specify both courses in the normal course by using a conditional statement, as discussed earlier. Your second choice is to specify one of the two courses in the normal course and the second as an alternative course. If you specify one of the two courses as an alternative course, you must identify the use case step at which the alternative course occurs and the use case step at which the alternative course rejoins the normal course. The choice is subjective. Try to determine which of the two choices is easier to follow and then document that choice.

A common mistake is to include two use cases in a single use case under the pretense of specifying an alternative course. We distinguish between the

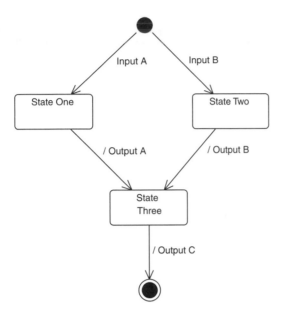

FIGURE 8.1
Alternative courses

two use cases and one use case with an alternative course on the basis of what the user perceives. The purpose of the use case is to change the state of the system to a desired state, produce outputs, or a combination of the two. If an alternative course achieves a different purpose, you most likely have two use cases. Alternative courses are usually numbered with the first number indicating where the alternative course branches from the normal course.

Exceptions and Issues

Exceptions in a use case normally result from either an unmet precondition or an error on the input. A use case is a set of actions that produces an output, changes the state of the system, or both. We specify the preconditions under which these actions apply. We also specify any inputs the use case receives. Under this concept, each step in the use case has these same attributes. Each step is an action that has preconditions representing the intermediate state of the system as the use case runs. Each step may also have input provided by the previous step. An exception occurs when the preconditions for the use case or the preconditions for any of the steps in the use case are not met. An exception also occurs if the input to the use case or the input to any of the steps in the use case is wrong.

You list exceptions in a separate part of the template. Our convention is to use the IF structure to specify a condition and the resulting system action. In this section, the tone is also conversational. For example, suppose a step in a use case requires as input the first name and last name provided by the user in a previous step. A missing first name or last name results in an exception in the use case. This particular exception is worded as follows:

If the first name or last name is blank, the system presents an error message to the user and requires the user to correct the entry or abandon the action.

The system response to the exception is another important aspect to consider. In the example above, the system requires the user to correct the entry or abandon the action. The system could just as well have warned the user and required the user to confirm the entry before continuing. You must specify the required system responses to exceptions in this section of the use case template.

Change Management Use Case

The Change Management System use cases have several examples that illustrate these points. The use case in Sidebar 8.1 allows the user, analyst, administrator, and project manager to view or edit an existing work request. The use case is a draft of what will become a final use case. Because the use case is a draft, it includes an item that is to be determined (TBD). Appendix B includes the full set of use cases.

SIDEBAR 8.1
USE CASE 2.2 VIEW/EDIT WORK ORDER

Created By: DW, RA
Date Created: April 29, 2001
Last Updated By: RA, DW
Date Last Updated: September 12, 2001
Actor(s):
User
Analyst
Administrator
Project Manager
Description:
This Use Case begins when the actor indicates the intent to view or edit a Work Order.
The system will allow only authorized changes by authorized personnel. This means
that changing the state of the request will depend on the role the actor is playing with
respect to the given system. The role of the Administrator will be allowed to make any
changes. If the type of Work Request is changed, the Work Request will be placed in the
Submitted state of the new type of request. This Use Case ends when the system has
presented the request and saved any edits made.
Preconditions:
The request exists in the system.
Postconditions:
Any changes made are saved to the system.
Priority:
High.
Normal Course of Events:
  1. The actor will indicate the intent to view/edit a Work Order.
  2. The system ensures that the user has the authorization to make the requested
      changes.
  3. The system presents the Work Order information to the user.
  4. The user changes, optionally, the TBD.
  5. The system saves the changes made by the user.
Alternative Courses:
None.
Exceptions:
None.
Includes:
None.
Notes and Issues:
None.

Using Storyboards to Validate the Use Cases

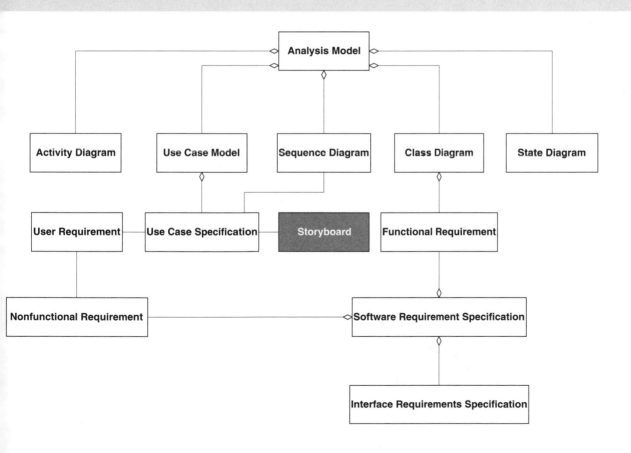

Presenting the use cases directly to the users is almost never an effective means of ensuring that the analyst and users have a shared understanding of the order in which actions must occur and what those actions must accomplish. We have found storyboarding to be far more effective at ensuring this shared understanding. In addition to presenting the storyboards, providing the use cases for review increases everyone's confidence in achieving this shared understanding.

In this chapter we define what we mean by storyboarding. We also offer ideas on how to develop and use storyboards. We then discuss the application of storyboarding to use cases. Finally, we look at a storyboard from our Change Management System.

Presentation of Storyboards to the User

A storyboard is simply a series of pictures from which a story is told. Normally, we arrange the pictures in a way that coincides with the sequence of events of the activity. We present a series of pictures that tells the story of what occurs, usually following a timeline. We have found that putting the requirements in terms of a story that is complete with pictures helps us achieve effective and accurate communications. The next question addresses the kind of pictures we might use in our storyboards.

Many developers immediately think of drawings of screen shots or screen images when thinking of storyboarding. User screens, in whatever form, tend to be an excellent way to help users visualize how the system will behave under a given set of circumstances. Once users can visualize the behavior along a timeline, it is easy for them to say whether that behavior is correct.

We can use other types of pictures in our storyboarding. These include flow charts, interaction diagrams, reports, and record layouts. Let's take a closer look at user screens.

Evolutionary Graphical User Interface Presentations

Some analysts show users a set of screens to be used in the application and ask the users to review the screens. We have found this process to be less effective than storyboarding. Users have difficulty determining whether a screen has all the necessary information without the context in which they will use the screen. Viewing the screens in the context of a function allows the user to determine whether the screen contains the right information for what the user is entering, the system is presenting, or the user is deciding.

For example, consider a screen that ultimately serves two purposes: order entry and order validation. If the screen allows the user to validate an order, the total price might be an important element for the screen. If, however, the user uses the same screen for order entry, the user might not think of the role the screen plays in order validation. The user might accept the screen, considering only order entry without considering order validation. The user would accept the screen with the total price information missing. Providing the context in which the screen is used helps ensure that the screen is appropriate for that use.

We have a number of choices about how to present screens. Drawing the screens provides an effective way to present the information content and available activities from the screen without implying any specific screen design. With today's advanced graphical user interface design applications, many analysts use prototyping. Prototyping can be accomplished in one of two ways: Throwaway and Evolutionary.

Throwaway prototyping is a method of developing prototypes as a communications vehicle. You never include Throwaway prototypes in the production system. This kind of prototyping has a number of drawbacks. First, you expend effort on an artifact that you simply throw away. Second, if you don't throw it away, you keep something you meant to throw away. This is especially bad because prototypes are not developed to be production code and often include poor-quality code. Evolutionary prototyping may be the better choice.

Evolutionary prototyping can be an effective choice for developing the screen shots for storyboards. Developers or analysts will take more care to write code to production standards if they understand they will include the prototypes in the production application. In addition, this approach allows you to apply the maximum amount of work to the production system. We have used Evolutionary prototyping a number of times and have had good success with it. However, Evolutionary prototyping has its disadvantages.

Evolutionary prototyping suffers from at least two major disadvantages. The first major disadvantage stems from algorithmic code that developers or analysts sometimes include in the prototype. The second disadvantage comes from setting user expectations for particular screen elements that are difficult to build in the production system. We discuss how each of these can lead to schedule problems and rework of the application.

The developer or analyst may expend a great deal of effort to include algorithmic code in evolutionary prototypes. This becomes a major problem when we are incorrect about the functionality the screen provides. We may have to throw all the algorithmic code away. Even worse, we may try to keep the algorithmic code and try to modify it to fit the newly found facts. This often leads to less than production-quality code. We believe you are better off including only navigational code and creating stubs to produce simulated results you would like to display. Throwing away the stubs is easy since they are only simulations and would not work in production anyway. Another problem with Evolutionary prototyping is the promise of more than you can deliver.

With today's modern development environments, developers and analysts can easily place sophisticated graphical elements on a screen. These elements tend to give our applications a professional look and feel. When users see the elements, the screen sets the users' expectations that these elements are no longer ideals but requirements. The problem arises when the developers have difficulty making the elements work in a realistic environment given the application. For example, displaying a table in modern graphical development environments is often easy. You even have a lot of choices for the look of the table. The table component may not be so easy to work with if the application must update each column. The component may be even more difficult to work with if you must be able to apply changes to multiple table rows that are not colocated. We are not suggesting that you don't use these components. We only suggest that you understand the graphical components and the effort to make them work under different conditions before including a particular component in a presentation to users.

Other Diagrams and Pictures

When storyboarding the requirements for a system with no graphical user interface or with functions invisible to users, you need to storyboard something other than User Screens. A number of other pictures can be useful in your storyboards. We have used Activity Diagrams, a type of flow chart, specifically for inclusion in a storyboard. With Activity Diagrams, we can examine each activity of a function in the context of all other activities.

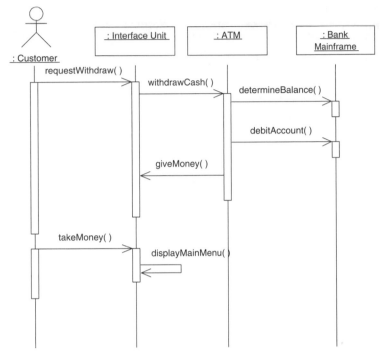

FIGURE 9.1
Interaction diagram

Another effective picture is the Interaction Diagram. We cover sequence diagrams as a type of interaction diagram in Chapter 13. For storyboarding in general, we simply mean a diagram representing specific elements of the system or interfaces to the system as vertical lines. The diagram illustrates the interaction between the elements as directed lines that connect one vertical line to another. The arrow indicates which entity initiated the action. Figure 9.1 illustrates an interaction diagram.

The example in Figure 9.1 illustrates how we might use an interaction diagram in our storyboarding. This example shows how the transaction of withdrawing cash from an ATM might proceed. A complete storyboard of this activity would include a screen image or drawing to show how the bank customer interacts with the system. The interaction diagram illustrates the interaction between the ATM and the bank mainframe after the customer has completed his interaction and is awaiting the money.

We could just as easily have used a flow chart. The choice of picture type is nearly limitless. We recommend working with whatever tool you find effective at communicating the information. Sometimes, communicating the timing of events is crucial. In these cases, an interaction diagram may be more effective. In some cases, the general flow of activities is the most important aspect or branching logic must be communicated. In those cases, the flow chart might be the more effective tool. Ensuring a shared understanding of the behavior is the true goal. This goal should drive your selection of the presentation images. Although storyboards apply to many situations, we are most concerned with validation of our use cases.

Presentation of Use Cases to the User

Our goal is to communicate the use cases to the user to obtain a shared understanding of the functionality the application will provide. Expect to have at least one storyboard for each use case. You may need multiple storyboards for use cases that include significant branching logic or alternative courses. Each storyboard should tell the story of the use case. Some use cases will require only one screen to tell the story; you display the screen and walk through the use case one step at a time. More often, a use case will require multiple screens; you walk through the screens as you step through the use case, emphasizing when the user has a choice and how the choice is made.

Change Management Systems Storyboards

Next we present a storyboard for use case 3.1 Create Version of our Change Management System. This use case answers the need to add new versions to an existing system. You would normally show the screen and walk the user through the functionality in the context of the use case. The storyboard includes a script for the walk-through with the user.

Assuming you are logged in to the application, this is the screen you are viewing (Figure 9.2).

The user presses the Manage Release/Version Information button to indicate that the user wants to manage version information. The system presents the Version information screen (Figure 9.3) with System defaulted to the first system the user is authorized to work on, Current Phase defaulted to Analysis, and a listing of all Change Requests for the system that have not been assigned to a Version.

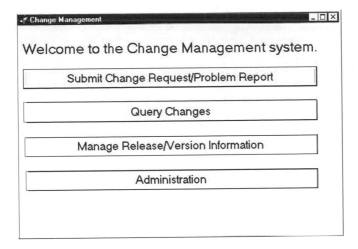

FIGURE 9.2
Screen One for use case 3.1

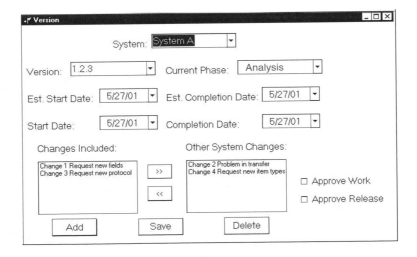

FIGURE 9.3
Screen Two for use case 3.1

The user must provide a Version Name and can also provide an Estimated Start Date, a Start Date, an Estimated Completion Date, and a Completion Date. The user can also select Change Requests to include in the version.

Upon completion of the version creation, the user presses Save.

Once the user has pressed Save, the system saves the version and associates any Change Request the user has selected to the version.

Building the Requirements Architecture

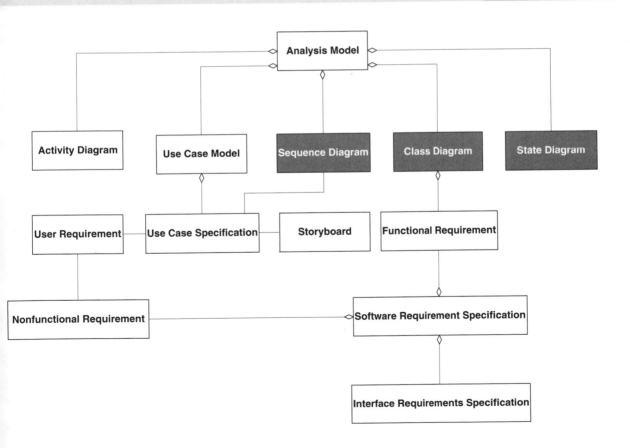

Entities and Events as Objects

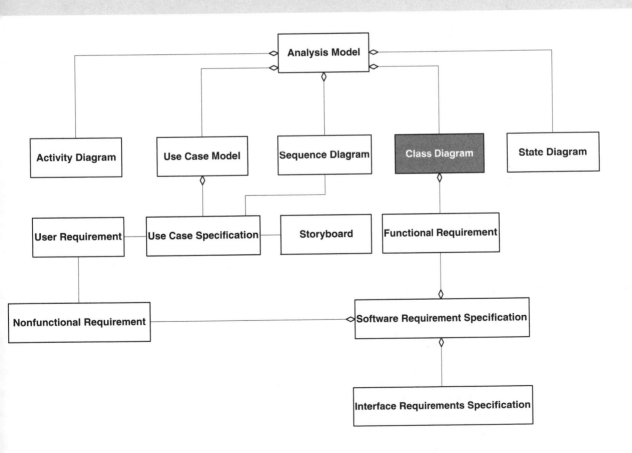

We build a model of the system as part of our analysis. We then use this model to ensure that we have a strong understanding of the software requirements necessary to meet the user requirements as represented by the use cases. We then use an analysis model as the basis for the remaining analysis. The analysis model is the central tool to move from analysis to design. The class diagram is the primary element of the analysis model.

First, though, we need to understand classes and their structure; we examine that in this chapter. We then work to understand the relationship between classes and objects. Finally, we look at an example from our Change Management System.

Classes and Objects

A class is a template for something that will exist in the application. This concept is similar to a pattern for a dress. You can use the pattern to create a dress or numerous dresses. The dresses have most things in common, but they may have different attributes or properties. For example, two dresses made from the same pattern might be made from different materials and be different colors. The class describes kinds of attributes or properties our objects will have. The class also defines the behaviors our objects will exhibit.

For example, we might create a class to represent the concept of a car in our system. We might need to represent any number of cars in our system, but we would expect each to follow the same pattern. A class consists of a class name, some number of attributes, and some number of methods. In the example in Figure 10.1, our class name is *CAR*. The example includes the attributes *NUMBEROFDOORS* and *SIZEENGINE*. The car example also includes the methods, or behaviors, *ACCELERATE* and *STOP*.

Naming things appropriately can help others understand the analysis model and help the analysis process. The class name should be descriptive of the thing being represented. The name should also represent a single entity, like the example. Similarly, we need to give our attributes and methods meaningful names.

Attributes represent properties of a class that must be remembered. Attributes are also referred to as fields or variables. Some attributes represent things that describe objects of this class, and other attributes describe the current state of the object. The example of the car in Figure 10.1 includes

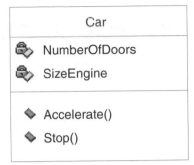

FIGURE 10.1
Car class

two attributes that describe the object that will be created from the class. Normally, an attribute is hidden from other objects and is only accessible from inside its object.

Information hiding is an important concept in object-oriented technology. Good information hiding requires the analyst to ensure that only the object has access to its attributes. Information hiding leads to systems that are more maintainable. Good information hiding also helps the analyst understand the dynamic behavior of the system by ensuring that the object maintains its own state. Attributes should only be accessible through the object's methods.

Classes define and specify methods that represent the behavior exhibited by objects of those classes. A method may represent a service the object provides to other objects, or it may represent internal functions to the object. Our car example has two methods. In this simple example, both behaviors represent services the objects of the car class provide. Methods can be fully specified in the analysis model, but full specification of methods is often left to the design model.

A fully specified method includes a return value type and a description of the information required by the method. If the method represents a function, the method would return a value when the method completes. The analyst would define the type of the return value. Additionally, the method may require information be passed to it. The information may be updated by the method. Again, the analyst would define the type of data that would be passed to the method in the class. Now that we understand classes, we need to understand objects.

An object is an instance of a class. Whereas the class was a template of a thing, the object is the actual thing that exists in the memory of the computer. We used the example of a car in Figure 10.1, when we described classes. Our class represented the idea of a car. We might create a specific instance of a car; a 2-door, 8-cylinder car would be an object of the type car. Given our class definition, we could ask our car to accelerate and stop.

Each attribute and method has an access specifier that constrains who can access the attribute or method. There are three levels of access: private, protected, and public. Access to a private attribute or method is usually limited to methods declared in the same class. A lock symbol represents private access. Access to a protected attribute or method is usually limited to methods declared in the same class or methods in derived classes (see Chapter 11). The key symbol represents protected access. Access to public attributes or methods is open to any method. A simple bar represents public access. Attributes and methods should always have the lowest access specifier possible to support information hiding and maintainability.

Let's look at one more example to reinforce our communication of the concepts. Figure 10.2 shows a class definition for a mammal.

Our application may require many mammals. We know that each object of the type mammal will include the attributes NUMBEROFLEGS and LIVING. Our objects also include the methods BREATH and ISALIVE. In this example, we included an attribute that refers to the state of object LIVING. We also wanted to practice information hiding, so we included the method ISALIVE. This method returns the state of our object without allowing other objects to directly access the LIVING attribute. We have also completely specified the class to give you a feel for what fully specified classes look like.

Our example shows the data types of our attributes. In the case of Figure 10.2, the attribute NUMBEROFLEGS is of type integer and LIVING is of type Boolean. We also specified the methods, including their return values and the information expected by each method. The method BREATH returns no value but requires the information LITEROXYGEN of the data type integer.

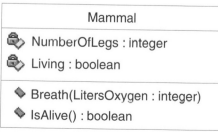

FIGURE 10.2
Mammal class

The method *IsAlive* tells the caller whether the mammal is alive by returning the state information from the attribute *Living*.

In our analysis, we model both static and dynamic views of the system. This requires us to understand both classes and objects. We use classes in our static model and objects in our dynamic model. But before we can consider modeling our problem domain, we need to find the things we will use in our model.

We will look in two areas to find the classes for our class diagram. Our use cases provide two important sources for classes. The first is the entities identified in the use cases. The second is the events specified in our use cases that we remember over time.

If you review the use cases for a system, you will find the specifications include entities. The entities are any person, place, or thing referred to by the use case specification. These entities represent strong potential classes.

Once we identify an entity, we ask two simple questions to determine if the entity should be a class.

What information must the system store about the entity?

What behaviors must the entity exhibit?

The entity makes a good class if your answers include several items. Otherwise, it is likely that the entity is simply an attribute of another class. Events we remember over time provide another potential source of classes. Consider a point-of-sale system. The use cases point us to a number of entities and events.

A point-of-sale system is concerned with a customer buying items from an inventory. We consider three entities from this simple statement. We can identify *Customer*, *Item*, and *Inventory* as potential classes. We may need to maintain information about our customers, so this appears to be a good class for our class diagram. We would certainly need information about the items we sell. So, *Item* appears to be an appropriate class. The *Inventory* class might need to provide the behaviors of inserting things and removing things from the inventory. If this were the case, we would include the class *Inventory* in our class diagram.

Remembered Events as Classes

We can look at an example in which an event remembered over time makes a good candidate class. In our point-of-sale system, we want to record all customer orders. An order would require us to relate a number of items to a specific customer request. This is an example of an event remembered over time. In the case of the customer order, we want to remember the date the order was made, the items that were ordered, and the total amount due for the order. The total price due for the order is an example of an attribute of the ORDER class. If you receive payment for the order, you would process the payment. This is an example of a behavior we need the class to provide.

Next, we look at examples from our Change Management System.

Change Management System Classes

In the Change Management System, the use cases contain many examples of entities. One specific example is the SYSTEM class, which we use to represent software systems. Figure 10.3 illustrates an example SYSTEM class.

A software system can consist of subsystems. Each of these subsystems is also a system. Our SYSTEM class includes the attributes NAME and PARENT. The NAME attribute uniquely identifies the system the object represents. The PARENT attribute points to the parent system if one exists. Each of the attributes is private and therefore only accessible from the SYSTEM object. The SYSTEM class also includes one method, GETSYSTEMS. This method is public and is a service other objects will call. The PERSON class, shown in Figure 10.4, is another example of an entity that we identified from the use cases.

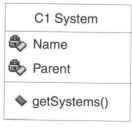

FIGURE 10.3
System class

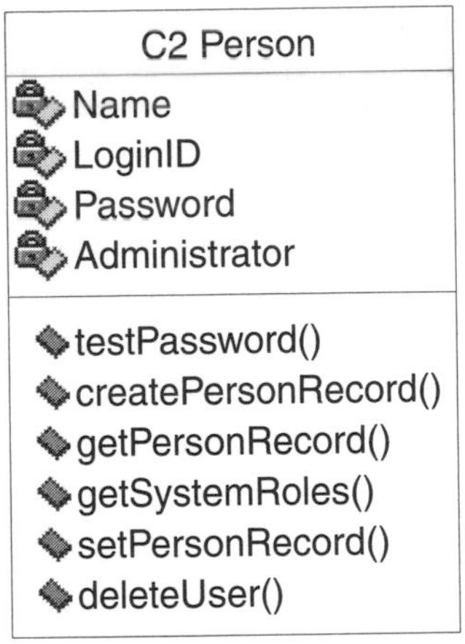

C2 Person
- Name
- LoginID
- Password
- Administrator

- testPassword()
- createPersonRecord()
- getPersonRecord()
- getSystemRoles()
- setPersonRecord()
- deleteUser()

FIGURE 10.4
Person class

The *PERSON* class is an entity that represents the persons that will use our system. The *PERSON* class has the attributes needed to ensure correct identification of persons. Notice that all attributes of the class are private. The *PERSON* class has a number of methods that make the class work effectively. These include the *TESTPASSWORD* method that ensures that the user is authorized to access the Change Management System. We also record the specific roles the person represented by the object may play. The *PERSON* object also allows us to add, edit, and delete persons from the system. We also have an example of an event that we want to remember over time.

Our system records each state change of a work request by creating a *CHANGEHISTORY* object, illustrated in Figure 10.5.

This object allows us to determine the current state of a change request. This object also allows us to determine the history of the change request. The *CHANGEHISTORY* class includes the private attributes *OLDSTATE*, *NEWSTATE*,

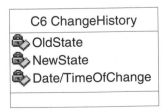

C6 ChangeHistory
- OldState
- NewState
- Date/TimeOfChange

FIGURE 10.5
Change History class

and *DATE/TIMEOFCHANGE*. We use these attributes to trace the history of all change requests throughout their lives in the system.

Now that we have a sense of what classes are and how to identify them, we need to learn how to use classes to model systems. The next chapter shows how relationships between classes enable us to use classes to model systems.

Building a Class Diagram

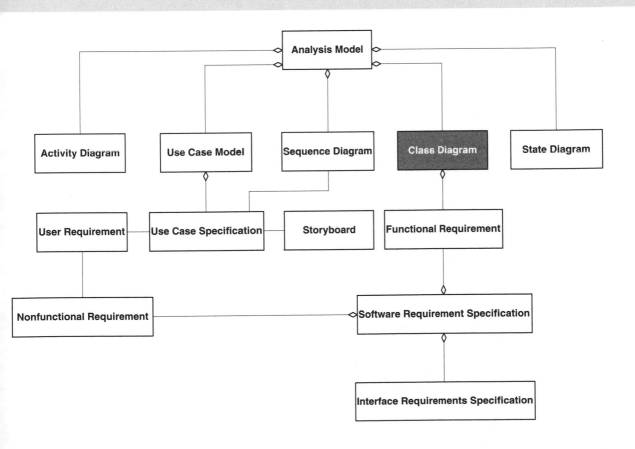

To build a class diagram, we must form relationships between classes. The three major relationships we must represent are, from the strongest relationship to weakest, generalization, aggregation, and association.

Generalization

Generalization is often referred to as inheritance. This is likely the hardest concept for people unfamiliar with object-oriented technology to understand, but it is an important idea. Generalization is the ability to create some base class and then have a derived class inherit the attributes and behaviors. We can make an analogy to the classification system used in biology. In this analogy, the animal class represents the base class. The animal class is a general classification. All animals have attributes and behaviors in common. For example, all animals have a circulatory system and breath oxygen. We could talk about a subclassification of animals: mammals. A mammal is a more specific category than animal. A mammal is a kind of animal. In fact, some refer to the inheritance relationship as an "is a" relationship. All the attributes and behaviors we attribute to animals, we automatically attribute to mammals. Mammals have some additional attributes and behaviors that may not be shared with all animals. For example, mammals are warm-blooded and have fur.

Figure 11.1 illustrates a simple system that contains three classes.

The three classes include the *SHAPE* class, the *SQUARE* class, and the *CIRCLE* class. The *SHAPE* class includes the attributes *AREA* and *VOLUME* and includes the methods of *GETAREA* and *GETVOLUME*. We provided methods only to get information from the objects of this class; we did not provide a way to set the information. This is appropriate because we do not intend to create objects from this class. We created the class only to allow us to inherit from it. A class created only to allow the creation of derived classes is called an abstract class.

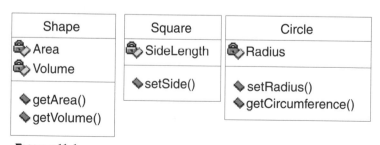

FIGURE 11.1
Shape sysem

Next, we have the class *SQUARE*. This class has the attribute *SIDELENGTH* and the method *SETSIDE*. The method *SETSIDE* calculates all other values we might want, given that a square has four equal sides.

The last class we included in this simple system is the *CIRCLE* class. This class includes the attribute *RADIUS* and the methods *SETRADIUS* and *GETCIRCUMFERENCE*. In this system, the *SQUARE* and *CIRCLE* class inherit from the *SHAPE* class to make them more valuable without repetition of the same things in two or more different classes. The inheritance tree is shown in Figure 11.2.

The triangle at the bottom of the *SHAPE* class signifies that the *SHAPE* class is a base class. The lines from the triangle run to the top of the *SQUARE* and *CIRCLE* classes. This means that the *SQUARE* and *CIRCLE* classes inherit the attributes and methods of the *SHAPE* class. In other words, if we were to create an object called *MYSQUARE* from the class *SQUARE*, the *MYSQUARE* object includes the attributes *AREA*, *VOLUME*, and *SIDELENGTH*. *MYSQUARE* would also include the methods *GETAREA*, *GETVOLUME*, and *SETSIDE*. We could execute the method *SETSIDE* that would set the length of a given side, calculate and set the area, and calculate and set the volume. We could get the area or volume by executing the *GETAREA* or *GETVOLUME* methods.

Inheritance can continue to as many levels as needed. There are many advantages to using inheritance in your software systems. First, you can

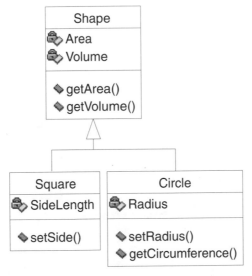

FIGURE 11.2
Shape inheritance tree

reuse code immediately simply by letting the code inherit from some base class. Otherwise, you might write the same code in two or more different places. Of course, you could cut and paste the code, but you would have to remember to implement any needed changes in every place you use the code.

Polymorphism

Inheritance enables another important concept in object-oriented techniques: polymorphism. Polymorphism is the ability of a program to call the same method on objects of different classes and have the class perform the appropriate function. Here we consider the example in Figure 11.3.

The base class in this example is the EMPLOYEE class. The EMPLOYEE class has the attribute NAME and the method CALCULATEPAY. The method CALCULATEPAY is an empty method that sets up the polymorphism. We call methods that are declared but not defined "abstract." Any class that includes an abstract method is an abstract class.

HOURLYEMPLOYEE and COMMISSIONEMPLOYEE inherit the EMPLOYEE class or are derived classes from the base class EMPLOYEE. Each derived class includes attributes and behaviors from the base class and those declared in the derived class itself. Both derived classes also redefine the method CALCULATEPAY. We could now build sets of employee objects and calculate each employee's pay without having to consider whether the employee is paid an hourly wage or earns a commission based on sales.

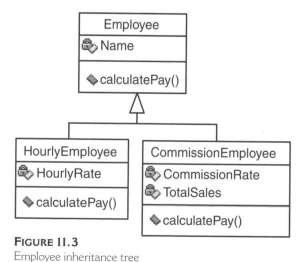

FIGURE 11.3
Employee inheritance tree

Polymorphism can make analysis, design and implementing object technology easier to understand. Polymorphism eliminates the need to write code that determines the type of object being used before calling the correct method. This is a real benefit when considering how error-prone that type of code tends to be.

Aggregation

The aggregation relationship is often referred to as the whole-part relationship. If we consider a car as a class, we could consider the engine and transmission as parts of the car. Many developers refer to this as the "has a" relationship. Figure 11.4 shows the aggregation relationship by using the diamond shape icon next to the whole in the whole-part relationship. The arrowheads indicate the way communications can occur. The absence of arrowheads indicates that communication occurs in both directions.

In our example, the whole class can call on the part classes, but the part classes cannot call methods in the whole class. It is normal for the whole to act as an interface to the parts of the component. In our example, the CAR includes the method DRIVE. If the method DRIVE were executed, it is likely that the DRIVE method would call the CHANGEGEAR method of the TRANSMISSION class. We might then execute the ACCELERATE method of our CAR class. The CAR class would then call for the execution of ENGINE method's INCREASEFUEL. The whole-part relationship is often used when a whole has a collection of parts.

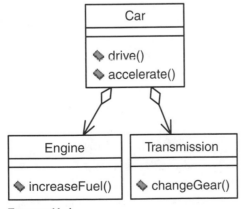

FIGURE 11.4
Car aggregation

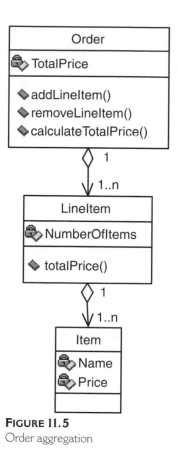

FIGURE 11.5
Order aggregation

Figure 11.5 shows another example of the whole-part relationship.

Our example in Figure 11.5 shows a whole-part relationship between the ORDER and a LINEITEM. We then have a second whole-part relationship between the LINEITEM and the ITEM class. In this example, we show the aggregation relationship by including the diamonds from the whole and a line to the part. We also show the navigability between classes with the arrowheads. We introduce the cardinality between the objects to be made from the classes.

The numbers next to our relationship lines show how many of one object are allowed to be related to another. In our example, we show a 1 next to the bottom of the ORDER class to indicate that a LINEITEM can be related to exactly one ORDER class. The 1..n at the top of the LINEITEM class means that an ORDER can have one or more LINEITEM objects related to it. The same is true between LINEITEM and ITEM.

Often, specifying the navigability and cardinality can help others understand the class diagram. These two characteristics of the relationship help explain the kind of communications required between given objects. The cardinality can also specify that a collection of parts is required. We never concern ourselves in analysis with the kinds of collection classes to use, but it is helpful to understand that often the entire collection must be used to answer questions. This point becomes clearer when we examine our example more closely.

The ORDER class has the attribute TOTALPRICE and the methods ADD-LINEITEM, REMOVELINEITEM, and CALCULATETOTALPRICE. The ORDER class can add and remove line items and can calculate the total price of the order. To know the total price, the ORDER class must know the price of each LINEITEM object. The LINEITEM object can calculate the price only by knowing the price of each item and the number of items included in the LINEITEM. This example illustrates one way the aggregation relationship is used.

Association

The association relationship is simply a relationship that means that two classes talk to one another. Often, one class provides a service to another class, or one class starts a series of events by executing the method of another class. The association relationship is the most common relationship between classes. The example in Figure 11.6 shows two association relationships.

The first relationship between CLASSA and CLASSB shows that the relationship has a cardinality of 1 to 1 or that a specific object of type CLASSA will be related to exactly one object of type CLASSB, and vice versa. The navigability indicated by the arrowhead tells us that an object of type CLASSA can call methods in the related object of type CLASSB. No object of type CLASSB can call methods in the related object of type CLASSA. The relationship between CLASSB and CLASSC is different.

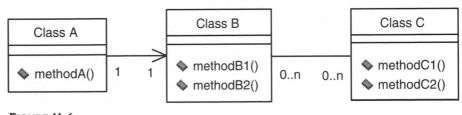

FIGURE 11.6
Class association

The relationships between objects of type *CLASSB* and objects of type *CLASSC* have a cardinality of 0..n to 0..n. This cardinality indicates that objects of type *CLASSB* can be related to as few as zero and as many as the computer can create of objects of type *CLASSC*. This same cardinality exists between objects of type *CLASSC* and objects of type *CLASSB*. In addition, objects of type *CLASSB* can call methods of objects of type *CLASSC*, and vice versa. You might think we should use arrowheads on both sides of the line to indicate bidirectional communications, but the UML has specified bidirectional communication as the absence of arrowheads.

Packaging Classes

When we build our requirements model, we will build several class diagrams. We will segregate our system into a model that covers the business logic. This is the model that is normally referred to as the problem domain model. In addition, we will build separate graphical user interface (GUI) class models. These models help us understand how the user will interact with the system. These models are often built in conjunction with a prototype. We often use an evolutional prototype of the GUI screens, as we mentioned in the storyboarding chapter. We would normally build one model for each unique set of GUI screens.

Next, we look at examples from our Change Management System. This system includes examples of the three relationship types we discussed. We take a look at some of those examples and discuss how the relationships allow us to effectively reflect the problem domain we are attempting to model.

Change Management System Examples

The group of classes shown in Figure 11.7 illustrates how we used the generalization relationship to help us model our problem domain.

In our example, the base class is the *WORKREQUEST* class. Our base class is intended to be abstract. In other words, an object of the type *WORKREQUEST* class will never be created. This class supports the concept that all requests for work will have common characteristics and behaviors. The *WORKORDER* and *CHANGEORDER* classes inherit the *WORKREQUEST* class' attributes and methods.

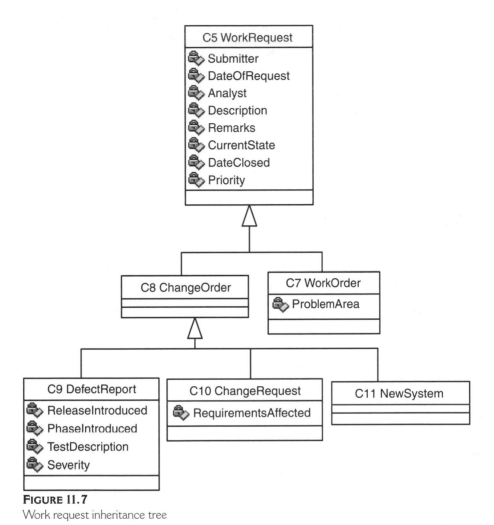

FIGURE 11.7
Work request inheritance tree

We use the WORKORDER class to handle any changes that do not require our software systems to change. Such changes include things like operating system configuration changes, operator errors, and errors in data configuration. The CHANGEORDER class models requests that require software changes.

The CHANGEORDER class is also an abstract class that acts as the base class to objects that reflect software work. Three classes—DEFECTREPORT, CHANGE REQUEST, and NEWSYSTEM—inherit from the CHANGEORDER base class. These classes represent the three possible requests for software work with which we must deal. This type of inheritance allows us to refer to each of these classes in a way that makes understanding the system easier.

In certain places we would like to refer generically to *WORKREQUEST*. No matter which actual type of request we are handling, it will be no problem to refer to it as a *WORKREQUEST* because of the inherited relationship each of these classes share. For example, in our Change Management System we have a *VERSION* object that includes one or more objects of type *CHANGEOR-DER*. In reality, the behavior of the *CHANGEORDER* will be similar once assigned to a release. Since each of the three types of objects that model the work we do in software are derived classes of the *CHANGEORDER* class, it is easy for us to work with any object of these types. We see how this relationship has helped our analysis in Chapter 13, when we will build a dynamic model of the system.

The example in Figure 11.8 shows the aggregation relationship.

This example shows that the *VERSION/RELEASE* class is the whole and that it includes the *CHANGEORDER* class as the part. We can see from the cardinality that an object of type *VERSION/RELEASE* includes one to many objects of type *CHANGEORDER*. We can also see that an object of type *CHANGEORDER* can belong to no object of type *VERSION/RELEASE* or the object of type *CHANGEORDER* can belong to exactly one object of type *VERSION/RELEASE*. This fact follows from the fact that a new change order may not have yet been assigned to a particular version of a system. However, once a change order is assigned to a version, it can be assigned to only one version of a system.

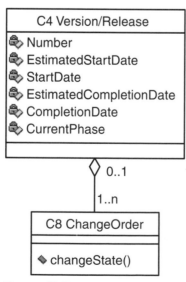

FIGURE 11.8
Aggregation of version to change order

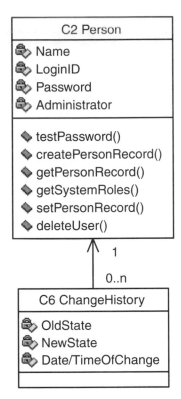

FIGURE 11.9
Relationship of person to change history

Figure 11.9 shows an association relationship.

Figure 11.9 shows that the PERSON class has an association to the CHANGE-HISTORY class. The cardinality of the relationship from the PERSON class to the CHANGEHISTORY class is 0..n, or, said another way, an object of type PERSON can be related to zero or many objects of type CHANGEHISTORY. The cardinality from the CHANGEHISTORY class to the PERSON class is 1, or, said another way, an object of type CHANGEHISTORY is always related to exactly one object of type PERSON. This follows because every change is made by exactly one person.

Using State Transition Diagrams

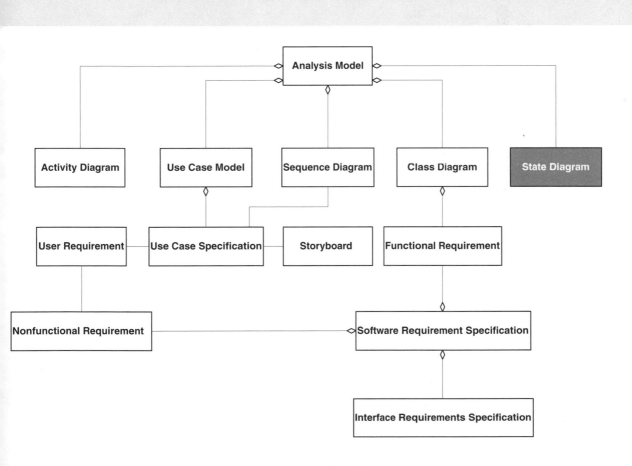

Introduction to State Transition Diagrams_____

State transition diagrams can be used to describe the behavior of a class, a use case, or a system. The key components of a state transition diagram are the states, triggering events that cause a transition from one state to another or possibly back to the same state, guards on those transitions, and actions the entity can perform when it transitions. The diagram in Figure 12.1 illustrates the notation.

A solid circle represents the START STATE. When the entity detects EVENT1, the entity checks to see if GUARD1 is true. If it is, the entity takes ACTION1 and then transitions from the START STATE to STATE ONE. If GUARD1 is false, the entity does not transition and therefore does not take ACTION1. The entity transitions out of STATE ONE on either EVENT2 or EVENT3, whichever occurs first, given that the appropriate guard conditions are met. If EVENT2 occurs first and GUARD2 is true, the entity transitions to STATE TWO and takes

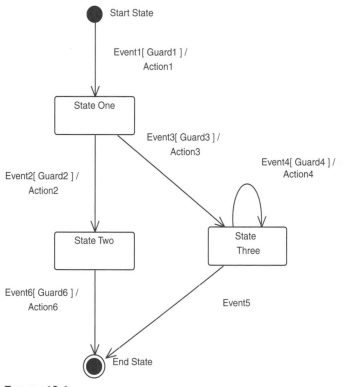

FIGURE 12.1
State transition diagram

ACTION2. If *EVENT3* occurs first, the entity checks to see if *GUARD3* is true; if it is, the entity transitions to *STATE THREE* and takes *ACTION3*. If it is false, the entity takes no action.

As illustrated in the diagram, an entity can take an action based on an event and a guard condition and then return to the same state. In this example, if the entity is in *STATE THREE* and it detects *EVENT4*, it checks to see if *GUARD4* is true. If it is true, the entity transitions back to *STATE THREE* and takes *ACTION4*. If it is false, the entity takes no action.

Guards and actions are optional. The state transition diagram may not specify a guard or an action. If no guard condition is specified for a transition, the entity transitions whenever it detects the specified event. If no action is specified for a transition, the entity transitions without taking an action. In Figure 12.1, if the entity is in *STATE THREE* and it detects *EVENT5*, the entity transitions from *STATE THREE* to the *END STATE* immediately without taking any action. One black circle inside another circle represents the *END STATE*. State transition diagrams must never allow an entity to transition to two different states from a given state as a result of the same event and guard condition (i.e., an event plus guard condition can only lead to a unique state). Finally, the entity ignores events if the state transition diagram does not specify a transition for an event in a given state. For example, if *EVENT1* occurs while the entity is in *STATE THREE*, the entity ignores *EVENT1*.

Class-Level State Transition Diagrams _____

State transition diagrams describe the behavior of entities. In the UML, entities include classes, use cases, and systems. State transition diagrams can communicate the complex behavior of any of these entities. In the Change Management System, the *RELEASE* class responds to stimulus very differently, in accordance with the value of the attributes that represent the *RELEASE*'s state at the time it receives the stimulus. The state transition diagram in Figure 12.2 illustrates this class' states and the valid transitions between them.

The release starts in the state *RELEASE CREATED*. In this state, the *RELEASE* class has an identifier and exists in the Change Management System. Once the analyst completes the analysis of all change requests associated with the release, the Project Manager sets the Release's estimated start date and estimated completion date. The Release is now in the *ANALYSIS COMPLETE* state.

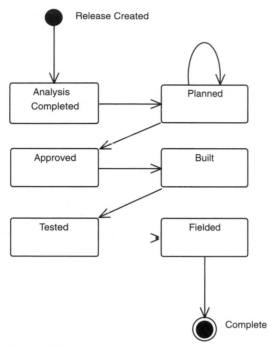

FIGURE 12.2
Class-level state transition diagram

Once the estimate is completed for the release, the Project Manager sets the Release's start date, updates the estimated completion date, and sets the current phase. The RELEASE is now in the PLANNED state. The Project Manager can change the estimated completion date. This transition leads from the PLANNED state back to the PLANNED state.

The Change Control Board (CCB) then reviews the Release contents and plan. Once the CCB approves the Release, the CCB sets the status of the Release to APPROVED. The development team works the changes into the release. The Project Manager changes the Release's current phase and the Release is now BUILT.

The Project Manager, in coordination with the Test Manager, conducts the testing of all the changes in the system. When the testing is complete, the Project Manager changes the Release's current phase and the Release is now TESTED. The CCB reviews the test results and approves the release of the system. The Release is now FIELDED.

Once rollout is complete, the Project Manager sets the Release's completion date. The Release is now COMPLETE.

This state transition diagram requires that the design reflect an orderly transition of the *RELEASE* through its life cycle. For example, the requirements specify that a *RELEASE* cannot transition from the *PLANNED* state to the *FIELDED* state without first transitioning through the *APPROVED*, *BUILT*, and *TESTED* states. This reflects the process that organizations normally follow to manage software releases.

Use-Case-Level State Transition Diagrams

State transition diagrams can also clarify use cases. In the Change Management System, the use case to edit a change order contains numerous checks on the states of various entities in the system. You cannot, for example, cancel a change order that is not submitted. The state transition diagram in Figure 12.3 specifies the viable actions the use case can take in accordance with varying conditions of the system.

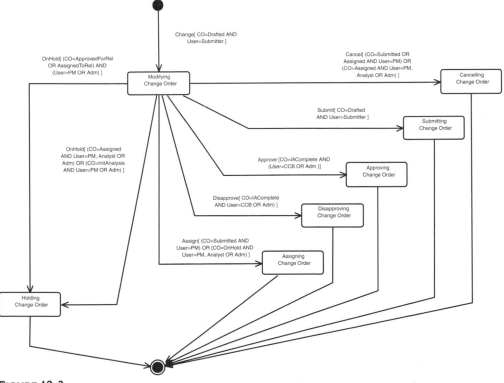

FIGURE 12.3
Use-case-level state transition diagram

The state transition diagram for the use case Edit Change Order describes the conditions under which a user can change the change order's status. You might find the text of the use case hard to follow. The state transition diagram, and even the process of defining the state transition diagram, clarifies the use case specification.

In Figure 12.3, you can see that the use case specification requires the user to be modifying a change order before the user can make any other changes to it. Further, the use case limits the changes the user is allowed to make; these restrictions are based on the authorization level of the user and the current state of the change order. For example, the state transition diagram shows that the system will cancel a change order in only one of two situations. The first situation requires that the change order has been submitted and that the user requesting the cancel be the Project Manager. The second situation requires that the change order has been assigned and the user requesting the cancel be the Project Manager, the Analyst, or the Administrator.

A second example from the state transition diagram involves approving the change for inclusion in a release. You can see from the diagram that only the CCB or the Administrator can approve the change order for inclusion in a release. Further, the change order must have had an initial analysis completed.

On the transition to the end state, the use case takes the appropriate action. The focus of this state transition diagram was on understanding when each type of action could be taken. Once this is clear, the action the system takes is relatively straightforward—the system changes the state of the change order and saves this information.

System-Level State Transition Diagrams

State transition diagrams are also useful at the system level. In most situations, you will be describing an aspect of the system associated with several uses that relate to each other. You rarely, if ever, model the complete state information for the entire system. The approach and notation remain unchanged for state transition diagrams at the system level.

Change Management System State Transition Diagram

The change order is the core concept in the Change Management System. Understanding the states and transitions of this class are central to understanding the requirements. As a result, we review this state transition diagram (Figure 12.4) in detail.

The *CHANGE ORDER* has ten states. A *CHANGE ORDER* that has been entered into the system but not submitted is in the *DRAFT* mode. A *CHANGE ORDER* that is in the system and ready for a Project Manager's action is in the *SUBMITTED* state. A *CHANGE ORDER* that has an Analyst identified to work on it is in the *ASSIGNED* state. A *CHANGE ORDER* for which an Analyst performed an impact analysis is in the *INITIAL ANALYSIS COMPLETED* state. A *CHANGE*

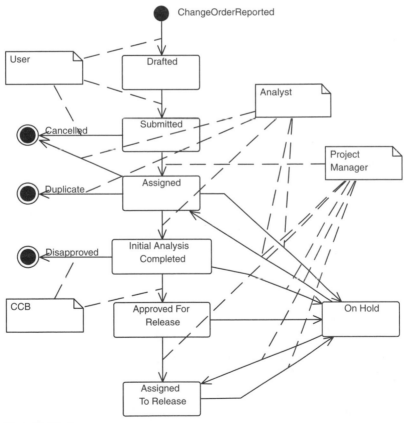

FIGURE 12.4
Change order state transition diagram

ORDER whose impact has been reviewed and approved by the Change Control Board (CCB) is in the *APPROVED FOR RELEASE* state. A *CHANGE ORDER* that a Project Manager has scheduled and planned into a release is in the *ASSIGNED TO RELEASE* state. In addition, the *CHANGE ORDER* may be *CANCELLED*, marked as a *DUPLICATE* of an existing *CHANGE ORDER*, *DISAPPROVED*, or placed *ON HOLD*. The state transition diagram specifies the allowable transitions between these states.

The state transition diagram starts with a user's submission of a change order. The *CHANGE ORDER* is initially drafted. In this state, only the user is allowed to complete and submit the *CHANGE ORDER*.

Once the *CHANGE ORDER* is submitted, the user can cancel it or the Project Manager can assign it to an Analyst for initial analysis.

Once the *CHANGE ORDER* is assigned, the Analyst controls it. The Analyst can cancel the *CHANGE ORDER*, place it on hold, mark it as a duplicate, or mark the *CHANGE ORDER* as having been initially analyzed.

When the *CHANGE ORDER* has been initially analyzed, the Project Manager can place it on hold or approve it. In this state, the CCB can also disapprove the *CHANGE ORDER* or approve it for a release.

After the *CHANGE ORDER* is approved for a release, the Project Manager can assign it to a release or place it on hold. The Analyst can take the *CHANGE ORDER* off hold and start initial analysis. Only the Project Manager has permission to take the *CHANGE ORDER* off hold and assign it to a release.

Use Case Realization by Means of Sequence Diagrams

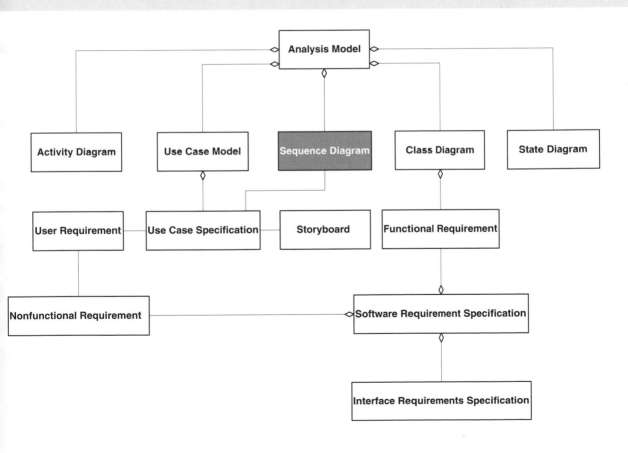

We use sequence diagrams to realize use cases in the analysis model. Before we demonstrate the realization, we need to have a good understanding of sequence diagrams. Sequence diagrams are a type of interaction diagram. Collaboration diagrams are another type of interaction diagram. Although each of these types of interaction diagrams provides the same information, the focus of attention is different. Collaboration diagrams focus on the objects that work together to accomplish a given task or series of tasks. Sequence diagrams focus on the interaction of a given task or series of tasks as observed over time. In fact, some modeling tools automatically convert one diagram to the other. In this chapter we focus on sequence diagrams since use cases model the services the system provides over time.

We discuss the elements that make up the sequence diagram. We then discuss how we map use cases onto a class diagram with sequence diagrams. Finally, we map a use case from our Change Management System onto the class diagram or analysis model of the Change Management System.

Introduction to Sequence Diagrams _____

A sequence diagram is a collection of objects interacting to accomplish a given task or series of tasks over time. Objects appear across the top of the diagram. A dashed line extends from the object to the bottom of the sequence diagram. Time is represented on the vertical axis. Methods that appear higher on the diagram occur earlier than methods that appear lower on the diagram. Figure 13.1 illustrates a sequence diagram.

Figure 13.1 shows a simple sequence diagram. In the example, an object of type *USER* triggers the occurrence of some event by calling the method *METHODA* in the object *OBJECTA* of type *CLASSA*. *METHODA* then calls the method *METHODB* in *OBJECTB* of type *CLASSB*. *METHODB* then calls method *PRIVATEMETHODB* within the object that contains *METHODB*.

The arrowhead points to the method that was called. Information can flow both ways. If the method is fully specified, as is the case for *METHODB* of *OBJECTB*, the information about the call is included in the method call. The return value is not shown in the sequence diagram.

The thick bar in the sequence diagram indicates the focus of control. Focus of control implies that one method called another; control will return to the first method. This focus can continue through any number of method calls. Focus of control does not always return to the calling method. Sometimes the new method starts a new thread of execution that takes the focus of control.

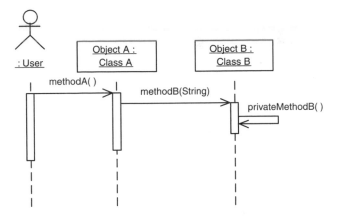

FIGURE 13.1
Sequence diagram

Recall from Chapter 11, that for a method from one object to call a method from another object, that object must have a public access specifier. Private methods can only be called by methods within the same object. Protected methods in a base class can be called by other methods declared in the same class or by methods that are declared in a derived class. If a method in a base class is defined as private, only methods declared in the base class can call that method. In Figure 13.2 we look at another example.

The example in Figure 13.2 shows an inheritance tree for an employee record. In the example, all objects of type *EMPLOYEE* include a method *PRINTRECORD*. The *EMPLOYEE* class also includes method *CALCULATEPAY* to allow polymorphism. Each of the derived objects—*HOURLYEMPLOYEE* and

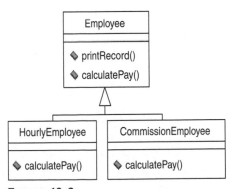

FIGURE 13.2
Employee inheritance tree

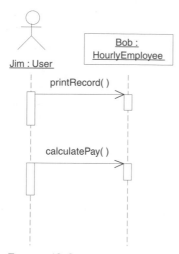

FIGURE 13.3
Employee sequence diagram

COMMISSIONEMPLOYEE—has its own version of the method *CALCULATEPAY*. We use objects from this set of classes in our next sequence diagram, Figure 13.3.

Figure 13.3 illustrates a sequence diagram that uses our Employee inheritance tree. We have instantiated an instance of a *USER* class and named the instance *JIM*. *JIM* initiates the method *PRINTRECORD* on the object *BOB*. The object *BOB* is of type *HOURLYEMPLOYEE*. *HOURLYEMPLOYEE* knows about the method *PRINTRECORD* because it inherited the method from *EMPLOYEE*. Next, *JIM* initiates the method *CALCULATEPAY* on our object, *BOB*. We can be assured that the correct *CALCULATEPAY* method will be called without regard to the derived type. This correct behavior appears natural in this example, but imagine if we had an array of objects of type *EMPLOYEE* with random objects in the array being of type *HOURLYEMPLOYEE* and the remainder being *COMMISSIONEMPLOYEE*. In that situation, we would depend entirely on polymorphism to determine the correct *CALCULATEPAY* to execute.

Realizing Use Cases in Sequence Diagrams_____

Realizing use cases by means of sequence diagrams is an important part of our analysis. It ensures that we have an accurate and complete class diagram. The sequence diagrams increase the completeness and understandability of our analysis model. Often, analysts use the sequence diagram to assign responsibilities to classes. The behavior is associated with the class the first time it is required, and then the behavior is reused for every other use case that requires the behavior.

When assigning behaviors or responsibilities to a class while mapping a use case to the analysis model, you must take special care to assign the responsibility to the correct class. The responsibility or behavior belongs to the class if it is something you would do to the thing the class represents. For example, if our class represented a table and our application must keep track of the physical location of the table, we would expect to find the method *MOVE* in the class. We also expect the object to maintain all the information associated with an object of a given type. Therefore, the *TABLE* class should include the method *WHERELOCATED*. This simple rule of thumb states that a class will include any methods needed to provide information about an object of the given class, will provide necessary methods to manipulate the objects of the given class, and will be responsible for creating and deleting instances of the class.

Another guideline helpful in building an analysis model is to examine the model from the whole-part perspective. The start of the sequence diagram is normally the most difficult aspect. It is important to have access to the object on which you will call a method to start the sequence. It is often the case that you will have to return to the whole to navigate through the whole-part relationship to arrive at the class you will be working with.

A simple example illustrates the whole-part relationship navigation. Suppose you were asked to read the first paragraph of three chapters of a book. First, you would need to know where to go to get the book. We might state that all books we are referring to are available at the Fourth St. library. You might then know to first go to the library, but the library has thousands of books. You might next have to consult the card catalog to determine where the book is located and then retrieve the book. Next, you might look at the book's table of contents to determine which pages concern you and then turn to those pages. We could consider the library as the whole and the books as the part of the whole-part relationship. The relationship between the book and the pages could also be viewed as a whole-part relationship. When we determined where to look and then proceeded to find that point, we were navigating the whole-part relationship.

Every time you find yourself navigating the whole-part relationship to find the appropriate class, you will need to assign responsibilities to the classes you are navigating to ensure that you can, in fact, find the appropriate class. Said another way, the navigating behavior must be a method on the class representing the whole. It is not unusual that this requires returning to the class that represents the system itself. Figures 13.4 and 13.5 illustrate this point.

The class diagram in Figure 13.4 shows three classes. Objects of type *POINTOFSALE* have zero to many objects of type *CUSTOMER.* Objects of type *CUSTOMER* have zero to many objects of type *ORDER.* Suppose the system

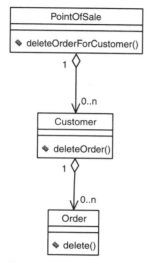

FIGURE 13.4
Whole-part class diagram

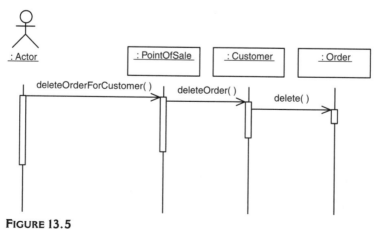

FIGURE 13.5
Whole-part sequence diagram

receives a message from an actor requesting that you delete a given order belonging to a given customer. The sequence diagram might look like the example in Figure 13.5.

The sequence diagram requires the system to navigate the whole-part relationships to delete the order specified by the object of type *ACTOR*. The sequence of events begins when the object of type *ACTOR* requests that a specific order be deleted for a specific customer. There is no way for the object of type *ACTOR* to call the delete method on the object of the type *ORDER* because the object of type *ACTOR* does not have a reference to the specific order. It is appropriate for the object of type *ACTOR* to have a reference to the object of type *POINTOFSALE*. This follows because there is only one object of type *POINTOFSALE* and it can, therefore, be referenced by name. The logical starting point for all interaction with the actor is the object of type *POINTOF-SALE*. The object of type *ACTOR* can then traverse the whole-part relationships to arrive at the specific object of type *ORDER* for which the action is intended. The responsibilities for navigating the whole-part relationship result in assigning behaviors to the object of type *POINTOFSALE* and the object of type *CUSTOMER*.

Example Sequence Diagram for the Change Management System _____

The Change Management System includes a method to create new versions for a given system. Figure 13.6 illustrates this activity by viewing the collaboration of objects required to accomplish this task with respect to time.

Figure 13.6 shows a sequence diagram from our Change Management System. In this sequence diagram, we assume the user has already logged in to the system. The example shows an instance of the *ACTOR* class, *JIM*. *JIM* begins the use case by requesting to work with versions, effected by clicking the Version Button. This action causes the *VERSIONSCREEN* object to be displayed.

Next, *JIM* indicates the intent to add a new version for the selected system by pressing the Add button. This action calls the *CLICKADD* method on the object of type *VERSIONSCREEN*. This method then triggers the screen's *CLEARFIELDS* method, which prepares the screen for the addition of the version.

The user then provides the appropriate information for the new version. Once *JIM* has provided all the information for the new version and clicks the Save button, the method *CLICKSAVE* is executed. The *CLICKSAVE* method calls

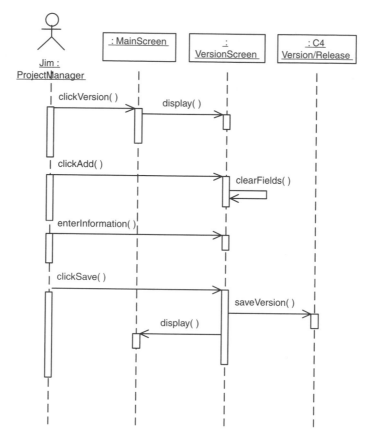

FIGURE 13.6
Create version sequence diagram

the method *SAVEVERSION* on the object of type *VERSION*. Once the new version is saved, the *CLICKSAVE* method of the object of type *VERSIONSCREEN* calls the *DISPLAY* method on the object of type *MAINSCREEN*.

This interaction ensures that our analysis model supports the use case Create Version. Once we have completed this mapping for all use cases in our Change Management System, we are sure that our analysis model fully supports our User Requirements. We are now ready to begin specifying the software requirements.

Building the Specifications

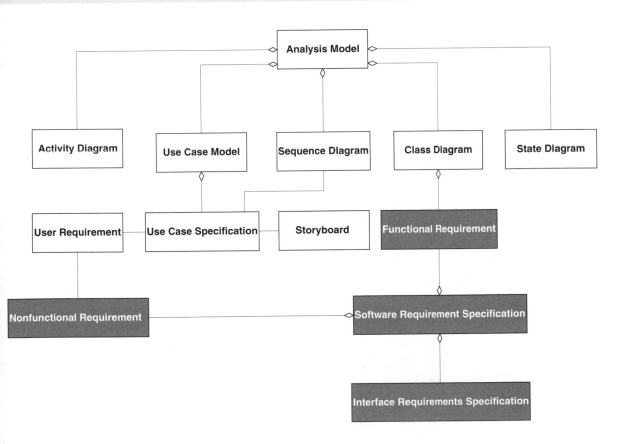

Developing a Software Requirements Specification

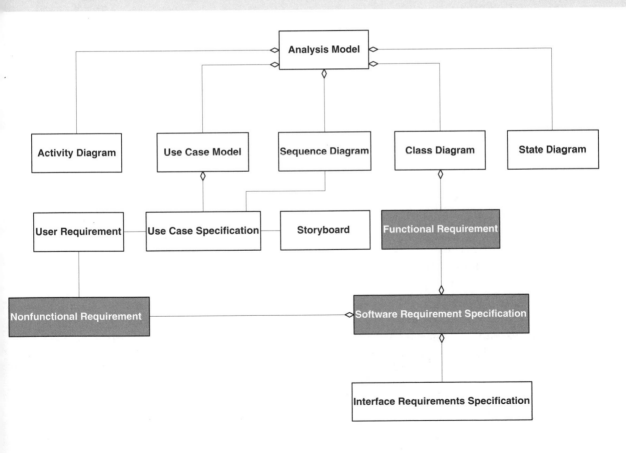

The Software Requirements Specification (SRS) has three main parts: the introduction to the document, the overall description of the system for which the SRS is written, and the specific requirements.

The introduction provides information about the SRS document itself. This information includes a statement of the purpose of the document, a statement of the system's scope, a list of definitions and acronyms used in the document, and a list of other documents referred to by this document. The introduction also includes an overview of the system for which the SRS specifies requirements. You must keep the statement of the system's scope consistent with any existing higher-level requirements documents. This means that if a system requirements specification, a concept of operations, or a vision document exists for the system you are specifying, you must link the two documents in this section. An acceptable method for providing this linkage is to list the high-level requirements to which this SRS applies. You can also cross-reference the higher-level requirements to the sections of this SRS that relate to them.

If the system interconnects with other systems as part of a larger system, the overview section of the introduction is the place to show that. A block diagram serves this purpose well. If the system stands alone, this is an acceptable place to include the system's context diagram. In some cases, you will want to include both a block diagram and a context diagram. In either case, you should avoid duplicating information that exists elsewhere. You can summarize and then reference the information. The SRS is similar to software: the more places you duplicate information, the more effort you must invest to keep the information consistent and correct and the more opportunity you provide to introduce errors.

The overall description provides a complete, abstract view of the system to which this SRS applies. The SRS specifies the software requirements. Business, user, and system requirements, when they exist, are specified elsewhere. The SRS provides a product perspective section so that you can describe this system in context. To this end, the overall description includes five sections: the Product Perspective, Product Functions, User Characteristics, Assumptions and Dependencies, and Apportioning of Requirements. We have included our tailored version of the SRS for our Change Management System.

Tailoring the Standard to Meet Your Needs _____

The standard for the SRS includes sections for numerous categories of information you might include when you specify the software requirements for a system. You will find that you do not always need every section. You can decide which sections to include through a process called tailoring.

You will tailor the standard across two dimensions. The first dimension involves decisions about which sections to include and to what depth to cover the information listed in that section. The standard itself describes content to three levels. You should not let this deter you from using the standard. Even experienced analysts profit from reviewing the standard to ensure that they have thought of all applicable information. As an aid, the standard walks you through all specification considerations for your system. Review each section and determine what information you need.

The second dimension of tailoring involves the organization of the core of the SRS. You specify the results of your analysis work in the Specific Requirements part of the SRS. This part makes up most of the document. All functional and nonfunctional requirements for the system you are specifying belong in this part of the document. The standard provides multiple means of organizing these requirements. These means include organization of the requirements by system mode, by user group, by feature, by functional hierarchy, or by classes and objects. You can also combine any of these for a hybrid organization. Our template reflects our choice of approach. We organize our template by classes.

Although we specify the attributes and methods of each class, we have tailored out the messages section of this part of the SRS. The standard includes a section for each class to list the messages that this class calls. This affords a list of all classes with which this class collaborates. We achieve the same result by making references to methods in other classes in the method that actually makes the call.

Specifying Functional Requirements from the Class Diagram _____

The analysis you have performed has resulted in an analysis model that fully describes both the structural and dynamic views of the software system you are specifying. Both views are critical to the understanding of what is required of the software to meet the users' needs. A critical benefit of our approach results from organizing the SRS such that we maintain both views.

There are two aspects to building the static view of the SRS. The first aspect is structuring the SRS. Our template leads you to organize the Specific Requirements chapter according to the class diagram. Each class has an entry in the table of contents. Each class also has a unique identifier. The procedure for building the structural view of the SRS is as follows.

1. *In your class diagram, label each class uniquely left to right, top to bottom. We recommend using "RN Cn," where RN identifies the entity as a requirement number, C identifies the entity as a class, and n is the class number you just assigned. The classes for the business classes start at 1. The classes for the graphical user interface classes start at 1000 and increment by 1000. This numbering guideline allocates room for frequent additions to the graphical user interface.*

2. *In your class diagram, label each attribute and method uniquely within each class. We recommend using "RN Cn-Am" for attributes and "RN Cn-Mm" for methods, where RN Cn identifies the class to which this attribute or method belongs, A identifies this entity as an attribute or M identifies it as a method, and m is a unique number you assign from top to bottom within the class.*

3. *Build the outline of the Specific Requirements section of the SRS according to this identification scheme.*

The second aspect of building the static view involves specifying each individual class, attribute, and method. First, we discuss specifying each class.

You use the class requirement specification to convey the intent of the class. For example, we have a class named WORKORDER in the Change Management System. This class represents a work order entered into the system. The requirement specification for this class might read as follows.

RN C7, Work Order *The Change Management System shall maintain a work order including a reference to the person who submitted it, the analyst assigned to analyze it, the collection of subordinate Work Orders that relate to it, and the collection of change histories associated with it.*

There are several key points to this requirement specification. The first is the use of the standard term "shall maintain." Recall that we discussed the use of standard terms in Chapter 2. We can see from the class diagram that WORKORDER maintains a reference to the submitter and analyst in its attributes. It also maintains a reference to all its change histories and to all other work orders that relate to it. We described these relationships in the requirement.

We specify the attributes by using similar concepts and phrasing. The WORKORDER class has the attribute PROBLEMAREA. In addition to specifying what the system does with this attribute, we specify the allowable values for this attribute. We also specify the default value. The specification for this requirement might read as follows.

RN C7-A1, Problem Area *The system shall maintain a problem area to identify the area to which the work order applies. The allowable values are point-of-sale system, warehouse management system, delivery system, and inventory system. The default value is inventory system.*

You should again notice the use of the key words to start the requirement statement. Also note the description of the purpose the attribute serves within the system. In this case, it is to "identify the area to which the work order applies."

Finally, you must specify the methods of each class. We use structured English in our approach. This aspect is similar to the standard we used for use cases; however, it is more formal in the SRS. This reflects the fact that the SRS is written in the language of the developers.

The fundamental elements of our structured English are sequence, iteration, and conditional logic. The last element requires the use of Boolean operators. We do not intend to introduce a standard for structured English. Any available structured English standard will suffice. However, we do describe how we apply this concept to requirements specification. The requirement statement for each method follows our standard phrasing. Any method specification that depends on state information checks the state information and proceeds accordingly. Finally, we clearly show any method specification that participates in collaboration with methods of other classes.

As an example, the SYSTEMROLE class has the method ADDSYSTEMROLE. The method ADDSYSTEMROLE sets the ROLE attribute for a given person on a given system. The attribute ROLE in the SYSTEMROLE class is an attribute with allowable values of user, analyst, project manager, CCB, and administrator. Its purpose is to identify the access level provided to the individual for a given system in the Change Management System. The requirement specification for the ADDSYSTEM method might read as follows.

RN C3-M1, Add System Role *The system shall set the role of the given Person to the given Role for the given System.*

You might notice the use of the word *given* in the requirement specification above. This requirement assumes that it is collaborating with a method of another requirement, perhaps in the user interface. It also assumes that the caller has given it the role, the system, and the person to whom it should assign the role.

As an additional example, the PERSON class has a method named TESTPASSWORD. The requirement specification for this method might read as follows.

RN C3-M1, Test Password *If the given password is equal to the stored password for this person, the system shall return true. Otherwise, the system shall return false.*

The example above specifies a conditional requirement.

Specifying Nonfunctional Requirements _____

Nonfunctional requirements are requirements that specify properties the software must exhibit. This is in contrast to functional requirements that specify actions the software must perform. Nonfunctional requirements include performance requirements, logical database requirements, design constraints, and software system attributes. The standard for Software Requirements Specifications, IEEE Std 830-1998, provides definitions and examples of these requirements.

Identifying Dependencies Between Requirements _____

In Chapter 2, we identified traceability as a characteristic of a good requirement. Building the dynamic view of the SRS involves specifying the dependencies between methods such that a reader can traverse the SRS according to all the sequence diagrams specified as part of analysis. Traditionally, traceability provides immense value when requirements change. Our method uses traceability to provide additional value during development. To understand the topic of this section, review the use of sequence diagrams, as described in Chapter 13. Recall that our process requires at least one sequence diagram for each use case. Also recall that these sequence diagrams represent how objects of the classes in our class diagram work together to realize each use case. From this point of view, these sequence diagrams represent dependencies between requirements. This section makes valuable use of building these dependencies into the SRS.

Each method in the SRS performs a specific function for the system. Each specific function is part of a larger collaboration within the system to meet a user requirement. We have already described these collaborations by using sequence diagrams. The procedure for including these collaborations in the SRS is as follows.

1. *For a use case, find the method in the SRS that starts the collaboration to realize the use case. Frequently, this is a method that receives a message, or this is a method linked to a user action on the user interface.*

2. *Identify the next method that participates in the collaboration. For example, to perform an operation on a member of a collection, you will frequently have to call the find method on the class that manages the collection.*

3. *Insert a reference—by unique identifier and name—to the method you are calling. If your word processor supports hyperlinks, use them.*

4. *Continue inserting references until the methods specified in the sequence diagram for the use case are included in the sequence of references.*

5. *Repeat steps 1 through 4 for each use case.*

Once you have completed the procedure for each use case, you will have built a dynamic view of the analysis model into the SRS. The value of the SRS increases dramatically. To review the specifics about how the system meets the use case, you traverse the entire set of collaborations that represent the use case realization. You now not only know the collaboration, you also have the details of all attributes and operations to give you a full understanding of the software requirements.

Two secondary uses of the SRS are simplified thanks to the structure of the document. The first use is by testers designing tests and building test cases (see Chapter 16). The second use is by analysts dealing with change as the system matures (see Chapter 17). We have included the SRS for the Change Management System as part of Appendix B to serve as an example of how you might create and maintain your SRS.

Developing an Interface Requirement Specification

In this chapter we look at the Interface Requirement Specification, or IRS. While the Software Requirements Specification (SRS) includes a section for external interfaces, there are times when you will want to write an IRS and simply refer to the IRS from the SRS, for example, when your system has numerous interfaces or when one or more interfaces are very large. Often, the people primarily interested in the IRS are not particularly interested in the SRS when building interfaces. Likewise, most people want to focus separately on these two issues: requirements and interfaces. Creating separate documents can help keep your SRS more readable. It is also possible that you will need to provide your interface specifications to developers of other systems, to enable them to build interfacing software. You may want to provide the interfaces without disclosing all the information available in an SRS.

The IRS Template

As of this writing (2002), the IEEE has not published a standard for the IRS. For this reason, we have chosen to use the specification developed and used by the Department of Defense (DoD) in standard Mil Std 498. The Mil Std 498 specifications are available from a number of sources on the Web. We significantly tailored the standard to fit our needs, but the military standard provided a good starting point. Figure 15.1 through Figure 15.3 illustrate the template as we tailored it. The accompanying text discusses what we would likely include in each paragraph.

Front Matter of the IRS

We begin the IRS with a title page like the title page in Figure 15.1. This page allows the user to identify the document and version of the IRS at a glance.

We also include a revision history page to communicate changes to the reader, as shown in Figure 15.2.

Figure 15.3 shows the table of contents from an IRS.

The table of contents shows that the IRS is organized into four sections: Scope of the document, References, Requirements, and Message Format.

The Scope section is organized into the subsections Identification, System Overview, and Document Overview. The Scope section tells the reader what the document is all about. The Identification subsection should tell the user to what versions of what systems the document applies. The System Overview subsection discusses the system that is being specified. This subsection should match the overview section of related documents like the SRS. The third subsection in the Scope section is the Document Overview. The Document Overview subsection should describe exactly what the reader could expect to find in the IRS. This should include all interconnected systems that are defined in the document.

Reference Section of the IRS

Section 2 of the IRS is the Reference section. This section includes a list of documents to which the IRS refers. The list is likely to include a System Requirement Specification and one or more SRSs. It might also include

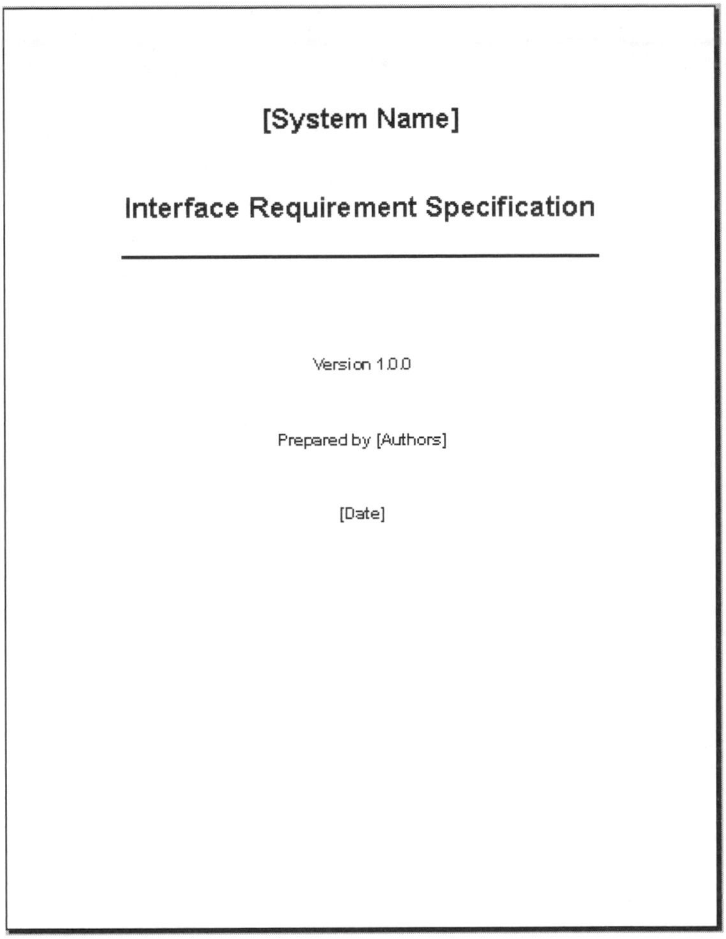

[System Name]

Interface Requirement Specification

Version 1.0.0

Prepared by [Authors]

[Date]

FIGURE 15.1
IRS title page

Request for Comments (RFC) that defines protocols like TCP/IP and SMTP. It may also include any other standards that define or specify protocols you are using.

Requirement Section of the IRS _____

Section 3 of the IRS is titled the Requirements section. This section gives the details of each protocol used. It lists each message that is interchanged with another system and includes a brief description of the message. Usually, we

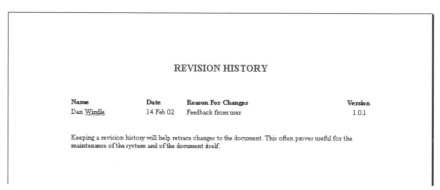

REVISION HISTORY

Name	Date	Reason For Changes	Version
Dan Windle	14 Feb 02	Feedback from user	1.0.1

Keeping a revision history will help retrace changes to the document. This often proves useful for the maintenance of the system and of the document itself.

FIGURE 15.2
Revision history

Table of Contents

FIGURE 15.3
IRS table of contents

would list a protocol and identify the systems with which we communicate by using the protocol. If we do not have a reference to explain the protocol, we specify the protocol element by element to ensure that our readers will be able to effectively implement the protocol. We repeat the protocol definitions for each protocol we use in our system.

The second subsection in section 3 specifies the messages. We usually create a subparagraph for each system. We list every message we send to that system along with a brief description of the message. We then list the messages we receive from the system along with a brief description of the message. We continue this until we have listed and described all the messages exchanged with all the systems with which our system communicates.

Protocol and Messages Section of the IRS _____

We use section 4 to specify all messages to the bit level. We make a subsection to discuss elements of the protocol. We create subparagraphs for each protocol that we specify. Each element of the protocol is specified individually. For example, we would define the header and trailer format used for the protocol. A checksum value might also be included in messages. The reader may need to know how to calculate the value. We also define the format of any acknowledgement messages. If the protocol uses a heartbeat message (a message that allows the system to know if the logical connection has been broken), we specify the format of the heartbeat message. We also specify any additional protocol elements the reader might need to implement to allow proper communications to occur.

Finally, the second subsection of paragraph 4 breaks down the informational messages that must pass between the system we are specifying and all other systems our system communicates with. We specify each message layout to the bit level. The format must provide all information the reader needs to successfully transmit the message to our system or receive the message from our system.

The IRS allows you to provide all the information readers need to understand and develop appropriate communications between systems without cluttering the SRS. You should consider developing one or more IRSs whenever you have complex or numerous interfaces to define.

Verifying the Software Requirements Specification

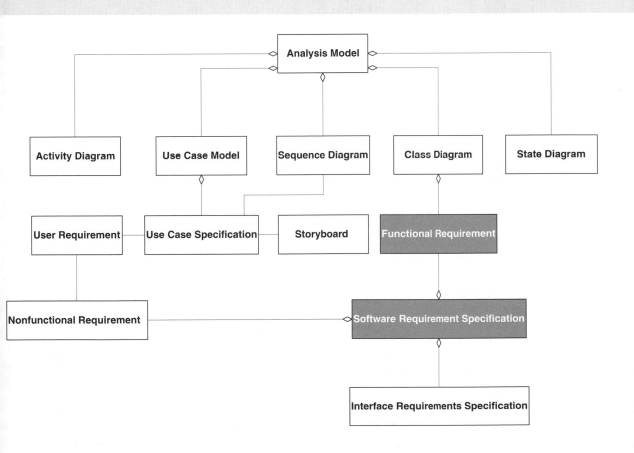

Through verification of the Software Requirements Specification (SRS), the analyst ensures that the SRS meets the characteristics of good requirements described in Chapter 2. These characteristics apply either to a single requirement or to the set of requirements. A single requirement should be unambiguous, verifiable, deterministic, traceable, and correct. The set of requirements should be complete, consistent, and modifiable. Ensuring that requirements exhibit these characteristics requires a combination of activities. The process and the notation minimize the negative aspects of some of these characteristics. Other characteristics require manual inspection of the requirements through a peer review. The remaining characteristics are often too complex to be verified solely in a peer review. For these, the analyst should apply some of the techniques used to develop specification-based tests.

Using the Process to Ensure Good Requirements

The process this book describes is designed to maximize the characteristics of good requirements. As described in Chapter 14, the SRS is developed directly from the class diagram. The structure of the SRS matches the structure of the analysis model. The dynamic view of the SRS matches the dynamic view of the analysis model. This minimizes the possibility of ambiguities introduced by the use of an informal representation.

Because the SRS maps directly to the analysis model, the process helps ensure that the set of requirements is correct and complete: correct, in that every functional requirement in the SRS is one the software must implement; complete, in that all necessary functional requirements are included. You ensure that every use case is realized in the class diagram through at least one sequence diagram. In this manner, the use cases drive the SRS. The SRS then includes all requirements necessary to implement all required user functionality. The SRS also includes only those requirements necessary to implement the required user functionality.

The process helps ensure consistency by requiring the specification of each attribute and each method in one place in the SRS. Collaborations that require state information reference the one definition. This minimizes the risk that a single attribute or action is specified differently in two different parts of the SRS.

Organizing the SRS according to the class diagram helps ensure modifiability. As you can see in Chapter 17, changes to requirements start at the use cases, proceed through the analysis model, and finally affect the SRS. The analyst finds changes required in the SRS by reviewing changes in the analysis model. Each attribute and each method are specified in one place to eliminate redundancy and increase modifiability.

The process reduces the chance that the negative aspects of these characteristics will affect the requirements. However, once the SRS is complete, a peer review ensures that the requirements truly embody these characteristics. Additionally, a peer review should ensure that the requirements exhibit some characteristics that the process cannot directly address, such as those described in later sections.

Using Peer Reviews to Ensure Good Requirements

A description of the peer review process is outside the scope of this book. We mention only that many acceptable peer review processes are available. These processes vary in formality from a desk check to a technical walk-through to a formal inspection. Whichever peer review process is chosen, the analyst responsible for the SRS must verify that the process actually ensured the characteristics we just discussed. Additionally, the peer review should verify several aspects of ambiguity, completeness, and verifiability.

Natural language ambiguities are minimized by the use of structured English in the SRS. However, it is impossible to determine whether two individuals will interpret a single statement differently unless each is asked. The peer review provides this insight.

The peer review must also verify the nonfunctional requirements. Given that nonfunctional requirements specify conditions or constraints on one or more functional requirements, they too, must be analyzed. The peer review should emphasize a review of the nonfunctional requirements to ensure that they are measurable, attainable, and testable.

Finally, the peer review must examine each requirement for two particular aspects of verifiability. The first aspect is the use of concrete terms. The words "may," "might, "should," and "can" in particular provide leeway in the interpretation of the requirement and should be flagged as suspect. The second aspect of verifiability the peer review must address is the use of measurable quantities when applicable. Key words that should raise suspicion in this respect include "better," "some," "sometimes," and "often." These two lists are by no means exhaustive, but they do illustrate the issue and provide a good starting point for collecting troublesome words.

Specifying a Test Tree_____

The list of characteristics of good requirements contains several items that are difficult to verify in a peer review. These include determinism, conflicts between specified actions, and testability. Additionally, backward and forward traceability requires work above and beyond the specification work. Our process uses techniques employed in building test cases, to ensure that the requirements exhibit these characteristics.

Verifying determinism requires ensuring that the system response to each input is specified under every applicable state of the system. To illustrate this concept, we reproduced as Figure 16.1 the whole-part example introduced in Chapter 13.

The class *ORDER* has the attribute *STATUS*. The order's status is open if no action has been taken on the order. The order's status is pending fulfillment if the order has been transmitted to the warehouse floor so that the items can be gathered and boxed for shipment. Finally, the order's status is filled if the items have been shipped.

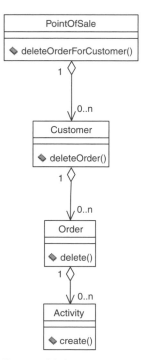

FIGURE 16.1
Point-of-sale class diagram

For our purposes, we have the class *ACTIVITY*. Objects of type *ORDER* have zero to many objects of type *ACTIVITY*. *ACTIVITY* records actions taken on the order. In this example, the use case *DELETEORDER* specifies how the user asks the point-of-sale system to delete a customer order. The specification for these requirements must consider the possible states of the system when this input is received. These include:

- Specifying the system response when the customer does not exist.
- Specifying the system response when the order does not exist.
- Specifying the system response when the order has already been filled.
- Specifying the system response under any other possible states of the system as represented by the state of the customer and the order.

The sequence diagram is shown in Figure 16.2.

The requirements for the methods identified in the sequence diagram might read as follows:

RN C1-M1, deleteOrderForCustomer

a. If the system does not find the customer, the system shall return the error "CUSTOMER NOT FOUND."

b. Else if the system finds the customer, the system shall delete the order (see RN C2-M1, deleteOrder).

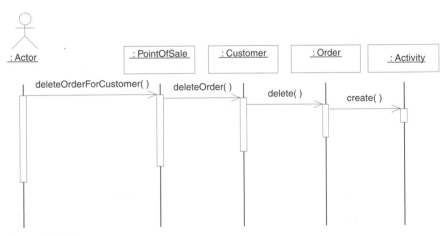

FIGURE 16.2
Point-of-sale sequence diagram

RN C2-M1, deleteOrder

a. If the system does not find the order, the system shall return the error "ORDER NOT FOUND."

b. Else if the system finds the order, the system shall delete the order (see RN C3-M1, delete).

RN C3-M1, delete

a. If the order status is open, the system shall create a delete order activity (see RN C4-M1, create) and return the message "ORDER XX, DELETED."

b. If the order status is pending fulfillment, the system shall create a tentatively deleted order activity (see RN C4-M1, create) and return the message "ORDER XX, PENDING DELETE."

c. Else if the order status is filled, the system shall create a too-late-to-cancel order activity (RN C4-M1, create) and return the error "TOO LATE TO DELETE."

RN C4-M1, create

The system shall create an order activity of the given type.

The sequence of actions specified above represents a flow of control through the system. Building a graph of this control flow helps the analyst understand whether the system specifies all possible system responses. One way of graphing the control flow represented by the above sequence is shown in Table 16.1.

TABLE 16.1
DeleteOrder Requirements Graph

From	To	Condition
Actor	RN C1-M1a	Customer Found
	RN C1-M1b	Customer Not Found
RN C1-M1a	Error	
RN C1-M1b	RN C2-M1a	Order Not Found
	RN C2-M1b	Order Found
RN C2-M1a	Error	
RN C2-M1b	RN C3-M1a	Order Open
	RN C3-M1b	Order Pending
	RN C3-M1c	Order Fulfilled

Continued

TABLE 16.1
DeleteOrder Requirements Graph (Continued)

RN C3-M1a	RN C4-M1
RN C3-M1b	RN C4-M1
RN C3-M1c	RN C4-M1

Analyzing the Test Tree

The table is an alternative representation of this portion of the specification. It shows the paths through the use case DELETEORDER. It also shows the test cases you would have to specify to test this functionality. To answer the question of determinism with respect to this use case, you must examine the table and answer the questions:

- Is the input required to arrive at each requirement specified?
- Is the action required before leaving each requirement specified?
- Is the action specified in only one place?
- Are there any conflicts between requirements in the sequence?
- Does the specification account for all states applicable to this situation?

In fact, if some of these questions cannot be answered, you cannot build the table. The table may be more easily visualized in a drawing. From the drawing, you might be able to more easily answer the questions listed above. It can also be represented as shown in Figure 16.3.

Whether you use a table or a drawing is a matter of preference. The table highlights issues the graph does not. For example, from the table, it is clear from the list of conditions on the order that we did not consider an order that has a pending delete or an order that was already deleted.

This example provides a technique for examining a single use case with the goal of ensuring that the requirements that realize the use case are deterministic. Realistically, most projects do not allocate the required time to allow an analyst to develop a full set of control-flow graphs or their equivalent table representations for every use case in the system. Given that the analyst may not be afforded the time to perform a complete SRS analysis with control-flow graphs, a less reliable but far quicker method is to create a single test case for each use case by traversing directly through the SRS. Developing a set of test cases for each use case by applying the above technique gives the analyst valuable insight into these issues. On most projects,

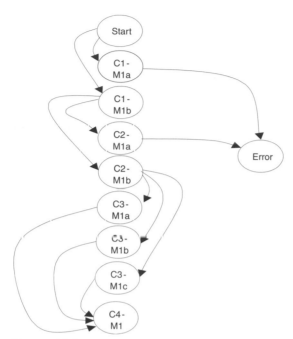

FIGURE 16.3
Drawing of Table 16.1

you would apply a combination of these two techniques. This means developing a test graph for the use cases that represent complex operations and using test cases directly from the SRS for the rest. The procedure for building the test cases is much like the example we just walked through.

The analyst traverses the requirements in the SRS for each use case. As each requirement is read, the analyst records the requirement number on the test case. Each requirement that is stated as a condition requires the analyst to choose—is the order open, pending fulfillment, or filled? The analyst records this choice as a precondition to the test case. Recording the requirements in the test case now serves two purposes. First, the analyst establishes traceability between the use cases and the SRS. Traceability is a characteristic of good requirements. Second, the analyst has recorded the state information in the preconditions. The analyst now knows what state information has not been specified in a test case. Once the analyst specifies all test cases, a comparison of the preconditions of the test cases with the possible values of the attributes as specified in the SRS convincingly checks the determinism of the specification. Finally, the analyst must think of a test procedure that executes the test case in a reasonable manner. This final check ensures the testability of the functional requirements.

Requirements Verification Checklist _____

Table 16.2 suggests checklist items that you can use to help ensure that requirements demonstrate the characteristics of good requirements.

TABLE 16.2
Requirements Checklist

Characteristic	Checklist Item
Correctness	Are all use cases realized through a sequence diagram?
	Are all requirements in the SRS also in the analysis model?
Unambiguous	Is there any use of the term "may," "might," "should," "can," "better," "some," "sometimes," or "often"?
	Are there any uses of other terms that are vague?
	Is your standard for structured English used consistently?
Completeness	Are all attributes and methods included in the analysis model also specified in the SRS?
	Are all conditions and constraints on functional requirements specified in the SRS?
	Have the test graphs and test cases been built and reviewed for this SRS?
	Are all references fully defined?
	Are all uncommon terms defined?
Consistency	Is each attribute defined once?
	Is each method defined once?
Verifiability	Are all quantities specified in measurable terms?
	Have test cases been defined for each use case scenario?
Modifiability	Does the structure of the SRS match the structure of the analysis model?
	Have all redundant structures been removed?
Traceability	Is each requirement uniquely numbered in a manner that allows the attribute or method to be associated with its class?
	Is each requirement traced to the use cases it helps realize?

Using the Requirements Architecture

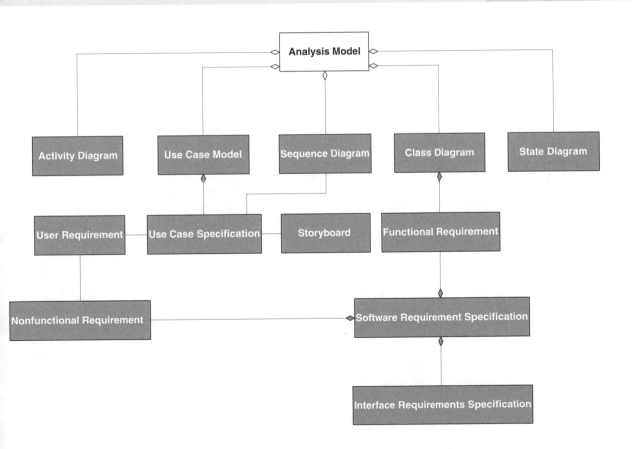

Maintaining the System

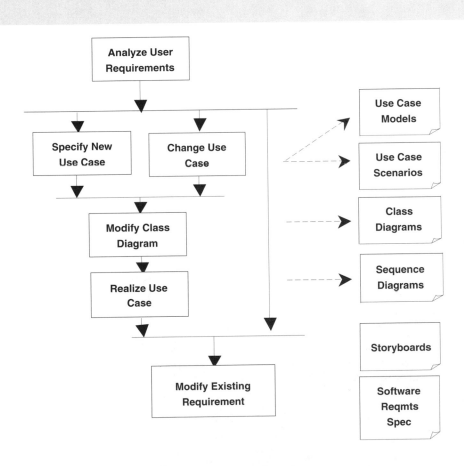

The majority of a software system's life is normally spent in maintenance. Maintenance work includes every change to the system after the initial release. This includes requests for enhancement, work to port the system from one hardware platform to another, or updating a protocol. It also includes fixing any defects discovered. In this chapter we focus on requests for enhancement. Changing hardware platforms normally impacts only nonfunctional requirements, and defects are usually the result of the system not meeting the requirements. Enhancement requests typically follow the process below.

1. *The change request is* PROPOSED.

2. *An analyst performs the initial analysis on the change request to determine an initial estimate of the size of the change and the effort required.*

3. *The CCB reviews the initial impact analysis and initial estimate and either* REJECTS, ARCHIVES, *or* ACCEPTS *the change request for the next release. If the change request is accepted for the next release, the program manager assigns the change to an analyst for full analysis.*

4. *While the change request is* IN PROGRESS, *the analyst performs a full analysis of the changes and issues a new estimate.*

5. *The CCB reviews the results of the full analysis and either* REJECTS *or* APPROVES *the change. If the change is approved, the program manager then includes the change in plans for the next release and assigns the change to an analyst for implementation.*

6. *The engineer implements the change as part of a release, and the reviewer tests the change to ensure that it is properly implemented. Once the change is fully implemented, the change request is* CLOSED.

Receiving the Change Request

This process begins when the customer or user submits a change request. The change request can be as simple as a color change to a label or the addition of a hot key. The change request can be a major new group of functionality that is as large as the existing system. It is important that the change request be properly managed. This process includes ensuring that the change request is assigned a unique control number and that the request is properly recorded.

We ensure that the change request includes descriptive text of the enhancements. Additionally, we ensure that the change request includes a table with each discrete requirement with a unique identifier that we can use to trace the changes through all the requirement artifacts that are affected.

Descriptive Text: The Change Management System will provide two reports to help study change history for a given system. This will include a report to provide the total number of defects reported on a given system. This report will provide a subtotal for year, broken down by severity. A second report will include the description of each change completed in the last year.

Table 17.1 summarizes the number assignment for the report requirements.

TABLE 17.1
Discrete Requirements

Requirement Number	Description
1	The system shall provide a summary report of defects on a given system.
1.1	The summary report shall be broken down by calendar year.
1.2	The summary report shall be categorized by severity of the defect within a calendar year.

Analyzing the Change

We want to take special care to analyze the change without compromising the requirements model. We have to consider that the change request may never be implemented or may wait a significant period of time before being implemented. Therefore, we normally work from a copy of the artifacts from the requirements model. We modify the artifacts as part of the analysis and maintain the copy we modified with the change request.

Often, the same processes used to analyze the original problem are useful in analyzing the change. There is, of course, one major difference. You now have in place the artifacts to analyze the change against. You may find it valuable to create a state transition diagram to explore the change. Activity diagrams are another way to diagram the change to help make the problem understandable. The best way to understand the change in context of the system is to use the requirements set you developed when the requirements were originally developed.

Analyzing User Needs

Once you have worked with the user to properly record and document the requirements, you will work with the user to ensure that you have a thorough understanding of what the user intends. This may require one or more interviews with the user. After you thoroughly understand the changes being requested, you can analyze the changes against the current requirements model. The process is illustrated in the figure that begins this chapter.

Identifying New and Changed Use Cases

You next review the use cases so that you understand the impacts. At this point, you should fully grasp the breadth of the user-requested change. With this knowledge, you can determine what use cases are likely impacted. You can probably now identify all the new use cases you will have to build. Once the use case is identified, you are ready to begin analysis. A good strategy is to attempt to identify the use case with the biggest impacts on the requirements model and write or rewrite this use case first.

While writing or rewriting the use case, consider all the other use cases related to this use case. If other use cases are included or are extended by this use case, review them to understand the impact that these changes will have on those use cases. Ensure that all impacted use cases are on your list of use cases to review. Also, examine any use cases that this use case is included in or is extended by. Ensure that the behavior specified in those use cases is not impacted. If the behavior is impacted, verify that those use cases are on the list of use cases to review.

You should continue with this procedure until you have examined all directly and indirectly impacted use cases. Be sure you make any changes necessary to a copy of the use case saved specifically for the change request being analyzed. Following this practice can save you from having to roll back changes if the change request is disapproved or placed on hold. Rolling back changes is especially difficult after modifications have been made for a number of change requests.

Identifying New and Changed Requirements

Additions and changes to the SRS are made through the analysis model and sequence diagrams. You will be tempted to make changes to the SRS in accordance with the changes you made to the use cases. Resist this temptation. The use cases, analysis model, sequence diagrams, and the SRS all provide a consistent view of the system. It is through the analysis model and sequence diagrams that you keep this view consistent.

Your first activity is to analyze the use cases against the analysis model to determine if you need to introduce new classes or, perhaps, remove existing classes. You may need to add additional attributes or methods to existing classes to support new functionality. Your second activity is to build a sequence diagram for each new use case. Your third activity is to revisit the sequence diagrams for each use case you changed. This activity may also lead to adding methods to existing classes. This process is iterative. Often the changes you make to realize new use cases in the analysis model will lead you to change related use case realizations.

These activities are likely to raise many questions. These questions often arise because the user did not specify enough information to make the changes deterministic. So these activities afford a valuable way to ensure that the user is aware of the effects the changes can have on other parts of the system. These questions can be fed back to the user in a number of ways. We usually make a list of questions we need answers to and any assumptions we made. If we can continue without the answers, we simply wait until we compile the complete list. Otherwise, we ask the user for any answers we need before we can continue. After the user has answered our questions and confirmed our assumptions, we present the user with storyboards that reflect our understanding of the change.

Once you have made the changes to these use cases and updated the class diagram and sequence diagrams, you should storyboard the changes back to the user to ensure his full and complete understanding. Storyboards for new use cases are developed as they were in Chapter 9. Storyboards for existing use cases should be focused on the aspects that have changed. It is important to talk about how the change added to and changed a use case. It is also important to point out any function that was provided but is no longer provided.

After we incorporate feedback into the requirements artifacts, we are ready to consider the change on the SRS. First, make a copy of the SRS to keep with the change request. We begin by making any changes to existing classes. Any attributes or methods added to our class diagram are added to our SRS. They must be specified to support our sequence diagrams. We may also have to change existing methods in some respect. We exercise great care that any modified methods still support other sequence diagrams that called the method. We also add any new classes. Of course, this may raise issues with other artifacts and begin another iteration to ensure that we have everything correct and complete.

Implementing a Release

Once a change request or a group of change requests are scheduled to be released in a version of the software system, we must update the Requirements Set. The update helps everyone understand the changes that will be included in the release and allows testers to begin preparing for the changes. We must update our use case models, update the use cases, and consolidate our sequence diagrams and class diagrams. Consolidating changes can raise conflicting requirements. All conflicts must be addressed with the user so that we understand the user's expectations, given the multiple changes that are being implemented. We also must update the SRS to represent all changes that are included in the release.

Ensuring Maximum Benefits from the Requirements

As discussed very early on, the process described in this book presents a disciplined approach to developing requirements. We have described how the use cases represent the user requirements and how the class diagrams, sequence diagrams, activity diagrams, and the state transition diagrams provide the analyst with the tools to ensure that the user requirements are represented by and consistent with the software requirements. We can now revisit the benefits of good requirements.

Benefits to Development and Productivity Revisited

The most visible benefit to this process is the ability to accomplish faster and higher-quality requirements analysis.

Benefit: A full set of requirements allows the analyst to identify up front all conflicts among user requirements. Identifying all unanswered questions and getting answers to those questions early saves the time and effort spent in building the wrong product and the time and effort spent reworking the products that were based on the poor requirements.

The process described in this book makes explicit the allocation of user requirements to software requirements. The analyst uses storyboards and prototypes to validate his understanding of the user requirements with the user. The analyst uses a set of class diagrams, sequence diagrams, and perhaps activity diagrams and state transition diagrams to ensure that inconsistencies between use cases are resolved before they are specified in the software requirements. The analyst also uses these tools to ensure that details not described in the use cases are specified in the software requirements. Finally, the analyst uses these tools to describe the requirements in the language of the developers who will design and implement the solution.

Benefit: A good set of requirements also represents a single source of a system's requirements. This means there is one place to find all the functions a system performs to meet a set of user needs.

The process in this book implements use cases to represent the user requirements. This process specifies the software requirements in a software requirements specification. Together with the various models, these provide a complete set of requirements for the software. A reader can see the full set of requirements from the user's point of view. He can then traverse the software requirements in the context of the use case by following the dependencies in the software requirements specification.

Benefit: A good set of requirements provides a foundation to begin design. A good set of requirements provides a direct mapping from the requirements as expressed in the language of the user to the requirements as expressed in the language of the developer.

The process described in this book provides a set of artifacts that express the software requirements both in the language of the user and in the language of the developer. The various models provide a direct mapping from the user requirements onto the software requirements. Because these models are the same types of models used for design, they provide a direct entry into the activities of the designer.

Benefits to Testing and Quality Revisited _____

A good set of requirements provides additional benefits to testing and quality. These benefits come from providing a tool for new team members to learn the system quickly and from providing a sound basis for testing the software.

Benefit: A good set of requirements helps decrease new team members' learning curve.

The process described in this book provides three views of the software. The first view is provided by the use cases. This view represents the system as seen through the user's eyes. The class diagrams provide the second view. This view is the structural view as seen through the software architect's eyes. The sequence diagrams provide the third view. This view provides a dynamic view from the developer's eyes by presenting the structure of the software and the collaborations among objects of the classes represented in the structure. The software requirements specification brings together both the structural view of the class diagram and the dynamic view of the sequence diagrams. Additionally, the software requirements specification presents the details required for the implementation. New team members can then quickly learn to use the system through the use cases while at the same time understanding the structure of the software through the set of class diagrams. Once new team members have the big picture, the software requirements specification allows them to delve into the specifics.

Benefit: A good set of requirements also allows for faster and more systematic testing.

The tester can learn the system much as a new team member would. The tester can then build test cases a use case at a time. This allows the tester to organize the use cases from the operational point of view. The software requirements specification, representing a control flow model of the system, allows the tester to specify test cases according to paths through the control flow that are based on specific inputs under specific conditions. The tester can then use the software requirements specification to predict the outcomes for each test.

Benefits to the Organization Revisited _____

Finally, a good set of requirements provides a safe store of a company's intellectual property. The initial functionality provided by the software, along with changes introduced over time, present a tremendous challenge to organizations facing constant pressure to shorten the time it takes to deliver new software releases in the midst of personnel turnover.

Benefit: A good set of requirements helps you understand the intricacies of the functioning of complex software systems both initially and as the requirements change over time.

The process described in this book ensures a full set of user requirements mapped to its full set of software requirements. The temptation with specifications is to consider them an after-the-fact description of the analyst's work. Such a view of use cases, class diagrams, sequence diagrams, and software requirements specifications will cause you to miss out on the benefits of a full set of requirements.

The process described in this book provides a set of tools and a set of practices for using those tools to actually perform the analysis. Understanding the changes required in the software requirements when you change a use case empowers you to change the requirements artifacts as you proceed. If you change a use case, the class diagram may no longer support that use case. The collaborations represented in the software requirements specification will most likely not realize the changed use case. As you make changes to the use case and the SRS, you will discover impacts in areas you did not consider when you first changed the use case. This interaction occurs during initial development and during maintenance of the software. Using these processes and artifacts gives the organization the added benefit of better initial performance and better sustained performance over time.

Appendices

A
Planning Model for Requirements Development

Model Work Breakdown Structure _____

Table A.1 lists the work breakdown structure (WBS) for the requirements development process described in this book. This table organizes the tasks by phase in a manner that describes two workflows: user requirements and software requirements.

TABLE A.1
Work Breakdown Structure

Phase	Task
Gather Requirements	Study domain
	Identify use cases
Analyze Requirements	Build initial class diagram
	Build sequence diagrams
	Build storyboards
	Externally review storyboards
	Rework
Specify Requirements	Specify use cases
	Specify attributes and methods
	Establish dependencies
	Review SRS

TABLE A.1
Work Breakdown Structure (Continued)

Phase	Task
	Specify interfaces
	Review IRS
	Rework
Verify SRS	Specify test cases
	Review test cases
	Assess use cases
	Assess class diagrams
	Assess SRS
	Assess IRS

Table A.2 describes the task network that integrates the user requirements workflow and the software requirements workflow into a single WBS for a project. The table lists the activity, the tasks that belong to that activity, and the dependencies between the tasks.

TABLE A.2
Task Network

No.	Activity	Task	Predecessor
1	User Requirements	Study domain	
2		Identify use cases	1
3		Build class diagram	1, 2
4		Specify use cases	3
5		Build sequence diagrams	4
6		Build storyboards	4
7		Externally review storyboards	6
8		Rework	7

TABLE A.2
Task Network (Continued)

No.	Activity	Task	Predecessor
9	Software Requirements	Specify attributes and methods	5, 8
10		Establish dependencies	9
11		Specify interfaces	5, 8, 9
12		Rework	15, 16
13	Requirements Verification	Specify test cases	12
14		Review test cases	13
15		Review SRS	14
16		Review IRS	11
17	Quality Assurance	Assess use cases	8
18		Assess class diagrams	8
19		Assess SRS	12
20		Assess IRS	12

Model Effort Allocation

Figure A.1 shows actual effort across the activities of the task network. The project was approximately 2500 function points. This project and six others yielded the effort allocation listed in Table A.3.

From the graph and the data table you can see that approximately half the effort is devoted to user requirements. Forty percent is devoted to software requirements. Twelve percent is devoted to verification activities associated with the software requirements, and six percent is devoted to independent evaluations of the artifacts and the process.

Our productivity averages 1.75 function points per hour for specification work. A large project of about 2500 function points consumes approximately 1500 hours. A medium project of about 1500 function points consumes approximately 1000 hours.

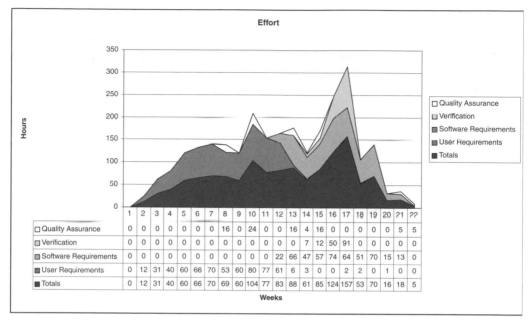

Effort

	1	2	3	4	5	6	7	8	9	10	11	12	13	14	15	16	17	18	19	20	21	??
☐ Quality Assurance	0	0	0	0	0	0	0	16	0	24	0	0	16	4	16	0	0	0	0	0	5	5
☐ Verification	0	0	0	0	0	0	0	0	0	0	0	0	0	7	12	50	91	0	0	0	0	0
▣ Software Requirements	0	0	0	0	0	0	0	0	0	0	0	22	66	47	57	74	64	51	70	15	13	0
▣ User Requirements	0	12	31	40	60	66	70	53	60	80	77	61	6	3	0	0	2	2	0	1	0	0
▣ Totals	0	12	31	40	60	66	70	69	60	104	77	83	88	61	85	124	157	53	70	16	18	5

Weeks

FIGURE A.1
Effort by phase

TABLE A.3
Effort Allocation

Activity	Percent	Effort (Large)	Effort (Medium)
User Requirements	46	690 hrs	460 hrs
Software Requirements	36	540 hrs	360 hrs
Verification	12	180 hrs	120 hrs
Quality Assurance	6	90 hrs	60 hrs

Model Schedule Allocation

Table A.4 shows how the effort was distributed across two analysts and one independent QA analyst. Figure A.2 shows schedule overlap among the activities.

TABLE A.4
Schedule Overlap

Activity	% of Schedule	% Overlap
User Requirements	62%	0%
Software Requirements	45%	14%
Verification	18%	100%
Quality Assurance	36%	100%

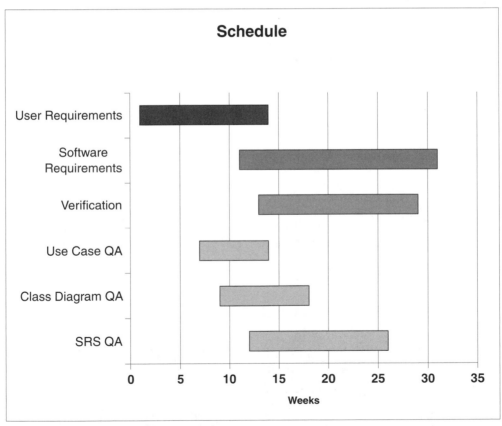

FIGURE A.2
Schedule

Standard Major Milestones_____

Table A.5 lists the milestones, defines them, and identifies the tasks from Table A.2 on which the milestone depends.

TABLE A.5
Major Milestones and Their Dependencies

Milestone	Definition	Predecessors
Use Cases Drafted	Use case models and specifications are written and internally reviewed by the requirements development team.	4
Sequence Diagrams Drafted	Each use case is realized in the class diagram.	5
Storyboards Complete	Storyboards are developed and internally reviewed by the requirements development team.	6
Requirements Gathering Complete	Storyboard reviews are complete. All defects, issues, and questions have been addressed. The use case models, use case specifications, class diagrams, sequence diagrams, and storyboards have been updated to reflect corrections.	8
SRS Drafted	The SRS has been specified and internally reviewed by the requirements development team.	10
IRS Drafted	The IRS has been specified and reviewed.	11
SRS Complete	The SRS has been peer-reviewed, and includes review of the analysts verification results.	12
QA Complete	An independent verification has been conducted of the use cases, the analysis model, and the SRS.	17, 18, 19, 20
Baseline Established	The use case specifications, the analysis model, and the SRS have been safely stored, uniquely identified, and released for general use.	17, 18, 19, 20

B

Change Management System Artifacts

This appendix begins with a complete use case set, including

- Title Page (framed, in this case)
- Table of Contents. The Table of Contents example also serves as a contents listing for the use cases presented in this section.
- Revision History
- Change Management Packages List. The packages list provides a higher level of abstraction before delving into the details.
- Use Cases

The second and third sections present Class Diagrams and State Diagrams for the Change Management System presented in the appendix.

The appendix ends with a complete Software Requirements Specification.

Together, these pieces illustrate the entire process described in the book.

Change Management System Use Cases _____

Use Cases

for the

Change Management System

Version 1

Prepared by D. Windle and R. Abreo

12 November 2001

Table of Contents

TABLE B.1
Revision History

Name	Date	Reason	Version
R. Abreo, D. Windle	4/29/01	Initial draft	Draft 1
D. Windle, R. Abreo	6/24/01	Add Normal Courses	Draft 2
R. Abreo, D. Windle	11/12/01	Add Use Cases; correct minor errors	Draft 3

Change Management Packages

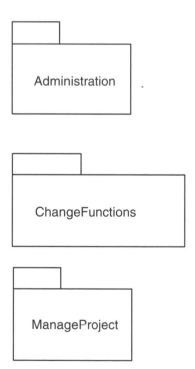

1. Administration

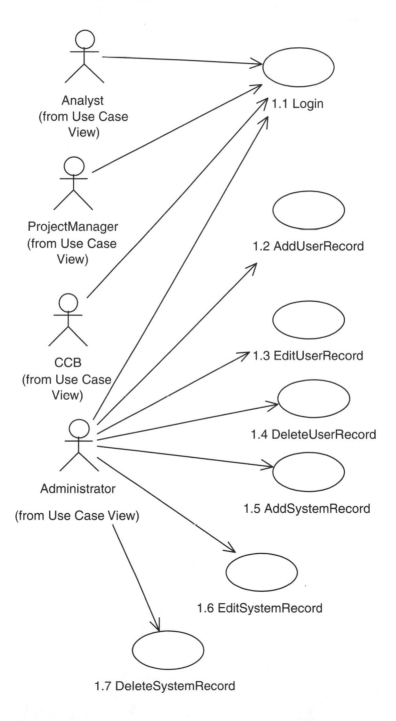

Analyst
(from Use Case
View)

ProjectManager
(from Use Case
View)

CCB
(from Use Case
View)

Administrator

(from Use Case View)

1.1 Login

1.2 AddUserRecord

1.3 EditUserRecord

1.4 DeleteUserRecord

1.5 AddSystemRecord

1.6 EditSystemRecord

1.7 DeleteSystemRecord

Use Case 1.1 Log in

Created By:	DW
Date Created:	April 29, 2001

Actor(s):

Administrator

Analyst

Program Manager

CCB

Description:

This Use Case begins when the actor indicates the intent to log in to the system. Every action in the system will require the user to log in. This Use Case ends when the user has been successfully authenticated in the system.

Preconditions:

The current user is logged in and authenticated.

Postconditions:

None.

Priority:

Low. (User Records could be modified directly in database.)

Normal Course of Events:

1. The actor will indicate the intent to log in to the system by starting the system.
2. The system will prompt the user to enter a user ID and password.
3. The actor will enter a user ID and password.
4. The system will verify the user ID and password.
5. The system will provide access to all appropriate functions.

Alternative Courses:

None.

Exceptions:

1. The user ID does not exist in the system.
2. The Password does not match the User Record.

Includes:

None.

Notes and Issues:

None.

Use Case 1.2 Add User Record

Created By:	DW
Date Created:	April 29, 2001

Actor(s):

Administrator

Description:

This Use Case begins when the Administrator indicates the intent to add a new user record to the system. This Use Case ends when the User Record is added to the system.

Preconditions:

The current user is logged in and authenticated as an administrator.

Postconditions:

The User Record exists.

Priority:

Low. (User Records could be inserted directly into the database.)

Normal Course of Events:

1. The administrator will indicate the intent to add a new user by selecting the Add User item from the Administrator functions.
2. The system will present the user with a screen for adding a new user and set the user default password.
3. The Administrator will complete the user ID.
4. The Administrator may also complete the following information
    4.1. E-mail address.
    4.2. Roles the user may participate in.
5. The Administrator will indicate the record is ready to be added.
6. The system will verify the User Record and add it to the system.

Alternative Courses:

None.

Exceptions:

If the user ID assigned already exists in the system, the system will reject the addition and require the administrator to assign a different user ID or abandon the action.

Includes:

None.

Notes and Issues:

None.

Use Case 1.3 Edit User Record

Created By:	DW
Date Created:	April 29, 2001

Actor(s):

Administrator

Description:

This Use Case begins when the Administrator indicates the intent to edit a User Record. This Use Case ends when the changes to the User Record are made to the system.

Preconditions:

1. The User Record exists.
2. The current user is logged in and authenticated as an administrator.

Postconditions:

The changes to the User Record are made.

Priority:

Low. (User Records could be modified directly in database.)

Normal Course of Events:

1. The Administrator will indicate the intent to edit a User Record by selecting the option from the Administrator functions.
2. The system will provide a list of current users.
3. The Administrator will select the record to work with.
4. The system will present the record in the edit screen.
5. The Administrator may modify the following information:
   5.1. Roles played by the user
   5.2. The user name
   5.3. The user e-mail address
6. The Administrator will indicate the changes will be saved.
7. The system will save the changes to the User Record.

Alternative Courses:

None.

Exceptions:

None.

Includes:

None.

Notes and Issues:

None.

Use Case 1.4 Delete User Record

Created By:	DW
Date Created:	April 29, 2001

Actor(s):

Administrator

Description:

This Use Case begins when the Administrator indicates the intent to delete a User Record. This Use Case ends when the User Record is marked as deleted.

Preconditions:

1. The User Record exists.
2. The current user is logged in and authenticated as an administrator.

Postconditions:

The User Record marked as deleted.

Priority:

Low. (User Records could be modified directly in database.)

Normal Course of Events:

1. The Administrator will indicate the intent to delete a User Record by selecting the record.
2. The system will present the delete option.
3. The user will select the delete option.
4. The system will verify the user's intent to delete the record.
5. The user will verify the intent to delete the record.
6. The system will remove the record from the system.

Alternative Courses:

None.

Exceptions:

None.

Includes:

None.

Notes and Issues:

None.

Use Case 1.5 Add System Record

Created By:	DW
Date Created:	April 29, 2001

Actor(s):

Administrator

Description:

This Use Case begins when the Administrator indicates the intent to edit a User Record. This Use Case ends when the changes to the User Record are made to the system.

Preconditions:

The current user is logged in and authenticated as an administrator.

Postconditions:

The system is added.

Priority:

Low. (User Records could be modified directly in database.)

Normal Course of Events:

1. The Administrator will indicate the intent to add a new system by clicking on the Administrator functions and then on the System functions.
2. The system will display the appropriate screen.
3. The Administrator will click the "Add" button.
4. The system will clear all information and present the "Save" and "Abandon" buttons.
5. The Administrator will add the appropriate information.
   Note: The user will be able to set a parent system for the new system.
6. The Administrator will click the "Save" button.
7. The system will save the record and present the screen appropriately.

Alternative Courses:

None.

Exceptions:

None.

Assumptions:

None.

Notes and Issues:

None.

Use Case 1.6 Edit System Record

Created By:	DW
Date Created:	April 29, 2001

Actor(s):

Administrator

Description:

This Use Case begins when the Administrator indicates the intent to edit a User Record. This Use Case ends when the changes to the User Record are made to the system.

Preconditions:

The current user is logged in and authenticated as an administrator.

Postconditions:

The system is added.

Priority:

Low. (User Records could be modified directly in database.)

Normal Course of Events:

1. The Administrator will indicate the intent to edit a system by clicking on the Administrator functions and then on the System functions.
2. The system will display the appropriate screen.
3. The Administrator will select the system record to be edited.
4. The system will display the system and present the "Save" and "Abandon" buttons.
5. The Administrator will change the parent of the selected system.
6. The Administrator will click the "Save" button.
7. The system will save the record and present the screen appropriately.

Alternative Courses:

None.

Exceptions:

None.

Includes:

None.

Notes and Issues:

None.

Use Case 1.7 Delete System Record

Created By:	DW
Date Created:	April 29, 2001

Actor(s):

Administrator

Description:

This Use Case begins when the Administrator indicates the intent to edit a user record. This Use Case ends when the changes to the user record are made to the system.

Preconditions:

The current user is logged in and authenticated as an administrator.

Postconditions:

The system is added.

Priority:

Low. (User Records could be modified directly in database.)

Normal Course of Events:

1. The Administrator will indicate the intent to delete a system by clicking on the Administrator functions and then on the System functions.
2. The system will display the appropriate screen.
3. The Administrator will select the system record to be deleted.
4. The system will display the system and present the "Save," "Delete," and "Abandon" buttons.
5. The Administrator will click the "Delete" button.
6. The system will present the confirmation screen.
7. The Administrator will click the "Confirm" button.
8. The system will remove the record from the system and present the screen appropriately.

Alternative Courses:

None.

Exceptions:

None.

Includes:

None.

Notes and Issues:

None.

2. Change Functions

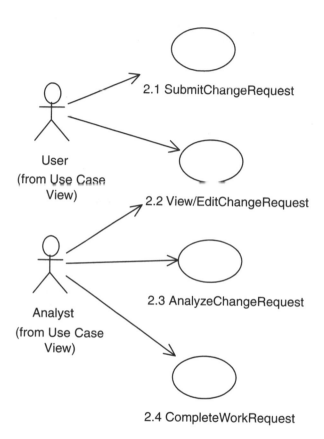

Use Case 2.1 Submit Work Request

Created By:	DW, RA
Date Created:	April 29, 2001

Actor(s):

User

Analyst

Project Manager

CCB

Description:

This Use Case begins when the actor indicates the intent to submit a Work Request. The system will present the appropriate form, based on the selected request type. This Use Case ends when the request is saved in the system and the system assigns a unique number to the request.

Preconditions:

None.

Postconditions:

The request exists.

Priority:

High.

Normal Course of Events:

1. The actor will indicate the intent to submit a Work Request.
2. The system will present the appropriate form for entering the Work Request.
3. The user may select a Work Request type from the list of types.
   Note: There are four types of Work Request—Work Order, Software Defect Reports, Change Request, and New System Request.
4. The system will present the appropriate fields for the given Work Request type with the Date of Request set to today's date, the Current State set to Drafted, and the System Name set to a designated system name.

4.1. If the Work Request is a Work Order, the system will prompt for the Submitter, Description, Remarks, Priority, Problem Area, and System Name.

4.2. If the Work Request is a Software Defect Report, the system will prompt for the Submitter, Description, Remarks, Priority, Release Introduced, Phase Introduced, Test Description, and System Name.

4.3. If the Work Request is a Change Request, the system will prompt for the Submitter, Description, Remarks, Priority, Requirements Affected, and System Name.

4.4. If the Work Request is a New System, the system will prompt for the Submitter, Description, Remarks, Priority, and System Name.

5 The user will complete the appropriate fields and either save as Draft or submit the Work Request.

6. The system will save the request and notify the user of the system-assigned request number.

7. If the user submitted the Work Request, the system will send e-mail to the system's manager.

Alternative Courses:

None.

Exceptions:

None.

Includes:

None.

Notes and Issues:

None.

Use Case 2.2 View/Edit Work Order

Created By:	DW, RA
Date Created:	April 29, 2001

Actor(s):

User

Analyst

Administrator

Project Manager

Description:

This Use Case begins when the actor indicates the intent to view and/or edit a Work Order. The system will allow only authorized changes by authorized personnel. This means that changing the state of the request will depend on the role the actor is playing with respect to the given system. The role of the Administrator will be allowed to make any changes. If the type of Work Request is changed, the Work Request will be placed in the Submitted state of the new type of request. This Use Case ends when the system has presented the request and saved any edits made.

Preconditions:

The Work Order to view/edit has been found.

Postconditions:

1. Any changes made are saved to the system.
2. The change history is recorded.

Priority:

High.

Normal Course of Events:

1. The actor will indicate the intent to view/edit a Work Order.
2. The system will present the Work Order.
3. The user makes the desired changes to the Work Order.

3.1. If the state of the work order is Drafted and the user is the Submitter, the system allows the user to change all the fields.

3.2. If the state of the Work Order is Drafted and the user is the Submitter, the system allows the user to change the state to Submitted.

3.3. If the state of the Work Order is Submitted and the user is the Project Manager, the system allows the user to assign/reassign the Work Order by changing the Current State to Assigned and changing the Analyst.

3.4. If the state of the Work Order is Submitted and the user is the Project Manager, the system allows the user to cancel the Work Order by changing the Current State to Cancelled and changing the Date Closed to today's date.

3.5. If the Current State of the Work Order is Assigned and the user is the Project Manager, the Analyst, or the Administrator, the system allows the user to cancel the Work Order by changing the Current State to Cancelled and to change the Date Closed.

3.6. If the Current State of the Work Order is Assigned and the user is the Project Manager, the Analyst, or the Administrator, the system allows the user to put the Work Order on hold by changing the Current State to On Hold.

3.7. If the Current State of the Work Order is Assigned and the user is the Project Manager, the Analyst, or the Administrator, the system allows the user to declare a Work Order a duplicate by changing the Current State to Duplicate and changing the Date Closed.

3.8. If the Current State of the Work Order is Assigned and the user is the Project Manager, the Analyst, or the Administrator, the system allows the user to change the Current State to In Progress.

3.9. If the Current State of the Work Order is On Hold and the user is the Project Manager, the Analyst, or the Administrator, the system allows the user to change the Current State to In Progress.

3.10. If the Current State of the Work Order is In Progress and the user is the Project Manager, the Analyst, or the Administrator, the system allows the user to put the Work Order on hold by changing the Current State to On Hold.

3.11. If the Current State of the Work Order is In Progress and the user is the Project Manager, the Analyst, or the Administrator, the system allows the user to declare a Work Order a duplicate by changing the Current State to Duplicate and changing the Date Closed.

3.12. If the Current State of the Work Order is In Progress and the user is the Project Manager, the Analyst, or the Administrator, the system allows the user to cancel the Work Order by changing the Current State to Cancelled and changing the Date Closed.

3.13. If the Current State of the Work Order is In Progress and the user is the Project Manager, the Analyst, or the Administrator, the system allows the user to declare a Work Order a duplicate by changing the Current State to Duplicate and changing the Date Closed.

3.14. If the Current State of the Work Order is In Progress and the user is the Project Manager, the Analyst, or the Administrator, the system allows the user to change the Current State to Completed.

3.15. If the Current State of the Work Order is Completed and the user is the Project Manager, the Analyst, or the Administrator, the system allows the user to change the Current State to In Progress.

3.16. If the Current State of the Work Order is Completed and the user is the Project Manager, the Analyst, or the Administrator, the system allows the user to change the Current State to Verified and to change the Date Closed.

4. The system will save the changes made by the user.

4.1. If the state of the Work Order has changed, the system will record a Change History to include the Old State, the New State, and the Date/Time of the Change.

4.2. If the state of the Work Order is Cancelled, Duplicated, or Verified, the system will assign the Date Closed.

Alternative Courses:

None.

Exceptions:

None.

Includes:

None.

Notes and Issues:

None.

Use Case 2.3 View/Edit Change Order

Created By:	DW, RA
Date Created:	April 29, 2001

Actor(s):

Administrator

Description:

This Use Case begins when the actor indicates the intent to view and/or edit a Change Order. The system will allow only authorized changes by authorized personnel. This means that changing the state of the request will depend on the role the actor is playing with respect to the given system. The role of the Administrator will be allowed to make any changes. If the type of Work Request is changed, the Work Request will be placed in the Submitted state of the new type of request. This Use Case ends when the system has presented the request and saved any edits made.

Preconditions:

The current user is logged in.

Postconditions:

1. The system has saved the changes added.
2. The change history is recorded.

Priority:

Low.

Normal Course of Events:

1. The actor will indicate the intent to view/edit a Change Order.
2. The system will present the Change Order.
3. The user makes the desired changes to the Change Order.
   3.1. If the state of the Change Order is Drafted and the user is the Submitter, the system allows the user to change all the fields.
   3.2. If the state of the Change Order is Drafted and the user is the Submitter, the system allows the user to change the state to Submitted.

3.3. If the state of the Change Order is Submitted and the user is the Project Manager, the system allows the user to assign/reassign the Change Order by changing the Current State to Assigned and providing/changing the Analyst.

3.4. If the state of the Change Order is Submitted and the user is the Project Manager, the system allows the user to cancel the Change Order by changing the Current State to Cancelled.

3.5. If the Current State of the Work Order is Assigned and the user is the Project Manager, the Analyst, or the Administrator, the system allows the user to cancel the Change Order by changing the Current State to Cancelled.

3.6. If the Current State of the Change Order is Assigned and the user is the Analyst, the Project Manager, or the Administrator, the system allows the user to put the Change Order on hold by changing the Current State to On Hold.

3.7. If the Current State of the Change Order is Assigned and the user is the Analyst, the Project Manager, or the Administrator, the system allows the user to declare a Change Order a duplicate by changing the Current State to Duplicate.

3.8. If the Current State of the Change Order is Assigned and the user is the Analyst, the Project Manager, or the Administrator, the system allows the user to change the Current State to Initial Analysis Complete.

3.9. If the Current State of the Change Order is On Hold and the user is the Analyst, the Project Manager, or the Administrator, the system allows the user to change the Current State to Assigned.

3.10. If the Current State of the Change Order is On Hold and the previous state was Approved For Release and the user is the Project Manager, or the Administrator, the system allows the user to change the Current State to Assigned To Release.

3.11. If the Current State of the Change Order is Initial Analysis Completed and the user is the Project Manager or the Administrator, the system allows the user to put the Change Order on hold by changing the Current State to On Hold.

3.12. If the Current State of the Change Order is Initial Analysis Completed and the user is the CCB or the Administrator, the system allows the user to disapprove a Change Order by changing the Current State to Disapproved.

3.13. If the Current State of the Change Order is Initial Analysis Completed and the user is the CCB or the Administrator, the system allows the user to schedule the Change Order by changing the Current State to Approved for Release.

3.14. If the Current State of the Change Order is Approved for Release and the user is the Project Manager, the CCB, or the Administrator, the system allows the user to schedule a Change Order by changing the Current State to Assigned to Release and assigning it to a release of a system.

3.15. If the Current State of the Change Order is Approved for Release and the user is the Project Manager or the Administrator, the system allows the user to change the Current State to On Hold.

3.16. If the Current State of the Change Order is Assigned Release and the user is the Project Manager or the Administrator, the system allows the user to change the Current State to On Hold.

4. The system saves the changes made by the user.

  4.1. If the state of the Change Order has changed, the system records a Change History to include the Old State, the New State, and the Date/Time of the Change.

  4.2. If the state of the Change Order is Cancelled, Duplicated, or Verified, the system will assign the Date Closed.

Alternative Courses:

None.

Exceptions:

None.

Includes:

None.

Notes and Issues:

None.

Use Case 2.4 Manage Change Order

Created By:	DW, RA
Date Created:	April 29, 2001

Actor(s):

Administrator

Project Manager

CCB

Description:

This Use Case begins when the actor indicates the intent to assign or un-assign a change order to a version/release. The Project Manager will assign a Defect Report to a Release. A CCB will assign other Change Order(s) to a release. This Use Case ends when the given Change Order(s) are assigned or unassigned from the given release.

Preconditions:

The current user is logged in and authenticated as an administrator.

Postconditions:

The system is added.

Priority:

Low.

Normal Course of Events:

1. The user will indicate the intent to assign a Change Order to a version/release.
   Note: The Change Order may be a Change Request, a New System Request, or a Defect Report.
2. The system will ensure that the user is authorized to perform the assignment.
3. The system will present the Change Order information to the user.
4. The user will provide a version/release identifier and changes the status of the Change Order.
5. The system will update the Change Order.

Alternative Courses:

None.

Exceptions:

None.

Includes:

None.

Notes and Issues:

None

Use Case 2.5 Query Work Orders

Created By:	DW, RA
Date Created:	September 17, 2001

Actor(s):

Administrator

Project Manager

CCB

Description:

This Use Case begins when the actor indicates the intent to query the system for a work order or a set of work orders. The user will be allowed to enter search criteria to limit the set of Work Requests returned. This Use Case ends when the set of Work Requests that meets the search criteria is returned.

Preconditions:

The current user is logged in.

Postconditions:

None.

Priority:

Low.

Normal Course of Events:

1. The user will indicate the intent to query the system for a Work Request or a set of Work Requests.
2. The system will prompt the user for the search criteria.
3. The user will provide the criteria.
4. The system will return the set of Work Requests that meet the criteria provided by the user.
   4.1. If the user specified an individual Work Request, the system returns that Work Request.
   4.2. If the user specified a System with a specified status, the system returns the Work Requests for that system with the status.

Note: The user may specify all open, all closed, or a specific status such as Drafted.

4.3. If the user specified a Release with a specified status, the system returns the Work Requests for the release with the status.

4.4. If the user specifies an Analyst or a Submitter, the system returns the Work Requests for the Analyst or Submitter.

4.5. If the user specifies a Work Request type, the system returns the Work Requests of that type.

Note: The type may be Work Order, Change Order, Defect Report, Change Request, or New System Request.

Alternative Courses:

None.

Exceptions:

None.

Includes:

None.

Notes and Issues:

None.

3. Manage Project

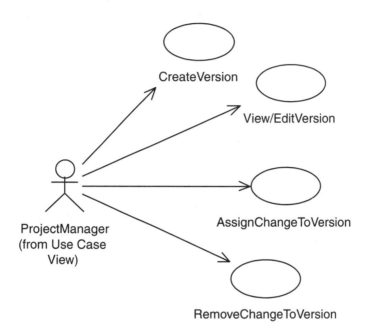

CreateVersion

View/EditVersion

AssignChangeToVersion

ProjectManager
(from Use Case
View)

RemoveChangeToVersion

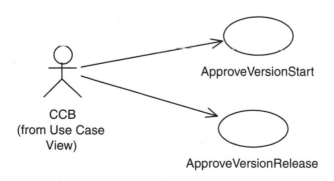

ApproveVersionStart

CCB
(from Use Case
View)

ApproveVersionRelease

Use Case 3.1 Create Version

Created By:	DW
Date Created:	April 29, 2001

Actor(s):

Administrator

Project Manager

Description:

This Use Case begins when the actor indicates the intent to add a new version or release to a system. The user creates versions of systems to implement Change Orders. Versions are created for individual systems and not for systems of interconnected systems. This Use Case ends when the new version is saved to the system.

Preconditions:

The actor is logged in and authenticated as a project manager.

Postconditions:

The version is added.

Priority:

High.

Normal Course of Events:

1. The actor will indicate the intent to add a new version by clicking the Create Version button from the main screen.
2. The system will present the version screen.
3. The actor will click the Add button.
4. The system will clear all fields, set the release status to Version Created, and set the Project Manager to the user.
5. The actor will complete the appropriate fields.
   Note: The actor will be required to input a system and a version number. The user may change the release status to Analysis Completed.
6. The actor will click the Save button.
7. The system will add the new version to the system.

Alternative Courses:

None.

Exceptions:

None.

Includes:

None.

Notes and Issues:

None.

Use Case 3.2 View/Edit Version

Created By:	DW
Date Created:	April 29, 2001

Actor(s):

Administrator

Description:

This Use Case begins when the Administrator indicates the intent to edit a version record. The user may change the release number, estimated start date, actual start date, estimated completion date, actual completion date, and the version status. This Use Case ends when the changes to the version record are made to the system.

Preconditions:

The current user is logged in and authenticated as an administrator.

Postconditions:

The changes to the version are saved.

Priority:

Low.

Normal Course of Events:

1. The user will indicate the intent to edit a version release of the system.
2. The system will present the version information.
3. The user may change the version release number, the estimated start date, the start date, the estimated completion date, the completion date, and the current phase.
4. The user will indicate the changes are complete.
5. The system will save the changes to the version release.

Alternative Courses:

None.

Exceptions:

None.

Includes:

None.

Notes and Issues:

None.

Use Case 3.3 Assign Change Orders to Version

Created By:	DW
Date Created:	April 29, 2001

Actor(s):

Administrator

Description:

This Use Case begins when the Administrator indicates the intent to edit a user record. The user may assign change orders to versions of systems. If the Change Order affects multiple systems, the user may initially assign the Change Order to a named system of interconnected systems, i.e., The Air Traffic Control System. Once the impact analysis is complete, the user may divide the Change Order into one or more change orders and assign each individual Change Order to a single system. This Use Case ends when the changes to the User Record are made to the system.

Preconditions:

The current user is logged in and authenticated as an administrator.

Postconditions:

1. The Change Orders are associated with the version.
2. The status of the Change Orders is changed to Assigned to Release.

Priority:

Low.

Normal Course of Events:

1. The user will indicate the intent to assign a set of Change Orders to a version release of a system.
2. The system will present all Change Orders that are approved for release or on hold and had previously been approved for release and are currently assigned to the system to which this version is assigned.
3. The user will indicate which Change Orders to assign to this version.

4. The user will indicate the assignments are complete.
5. The system will change the status of the Change Orders to Assigned to Release and will associate each Change Order with this version.

Alternative Courses:

None.

Exceptions:

None.

Includes:

None.

Notes and Issues:

None.

Use Case 3.4 Remove Change Order from Version

Created By:	DW
Date Created:	April 29, 2001

Actor(s):

Administrator

Description:

This Use Case begins when the user indicates the intent to remove a Change Order from a version. The user is allowed to remove Change Orders whose status is assigned to release from the version with which the change order is associated. This Use Case ends when the changes to the User Record are made to the system.

Preconditions:

The current user is logged in and authenticated as an administrator.

Postconditions:

1. The Change Order(s) are dissociated from the version.
2. The status of the Change Order(s) is changed to On Hold.

Priority:

Low.

Normal Course of Events:

1. The user will indicate the intent to remove one or more change orders from a version release of a system.
2. The system will present all change orders associated with the version.
3. The user will indicate which change orders to remove from the version.
4. The system will change the status of the change orders to On Hold and will dissociate the change orders from the version.

Alternative Courses:

None.

Exceptions:

None.

Includes:

None.

Notes and Issues:

None.

Use Case 3.5 Approve Version Start

Created By:	DW
Date Created:	April 29, 2001

Actor(s):

CCB

Description:

This Use Case begins when the user indicates the intent approve a version to start work. This Use Case ends when the version is marked as approved to start work.

Preconditions:

1. The current user is logged in and authenticated as a CCB.
2. The version exists.
3. The current status of the version is planned.
4. The version has at least one Change Order associated with it.

Postconditions:

The version status is set to "Approved to begin work."

Priority:

Low.

Normal Course of Events:

1. The user will indicate the intent to approve a version to begin work.
2. The system will present the version information.
3. The user will mark the version as approved for work.
4. The system will change the status of the version to "Approved to begin work."

Alternative Courses:

None.

Exceptions:

None.

Includes:

None.

Notes and Issues:

None.

Use Case 3.6 Approve Version Release

Created By:	DW
Date Created:	April 29, 2001

Actor(s):

CCB

Description:

This Use Case begins when the user indicates the intent to approve a version for release to production. This Use Case ends when the version is marked as Approved to Release to Production.

Preconditions:

1. The current user is logged in and authenticated as a CCB.
2. The version exists.
3. The version status is "Tested."
4. The version has at least one Change Order associated with it.

Postconditions:

The version status is set to "Approved to Release."

Priority:

Low.

Normal Course of Events:

1. The user will indicate the intent to approve a version to release.
2. The system will present the version information.
3. The user will mark the version as approved to release.
4. The system will change the status of the version to "Approved to Release."

Alternative Courses:

None.

Exceptions:

None.

Includes:

None.

Notes and Issues:

None.

Change Management System Class Diagrams_____

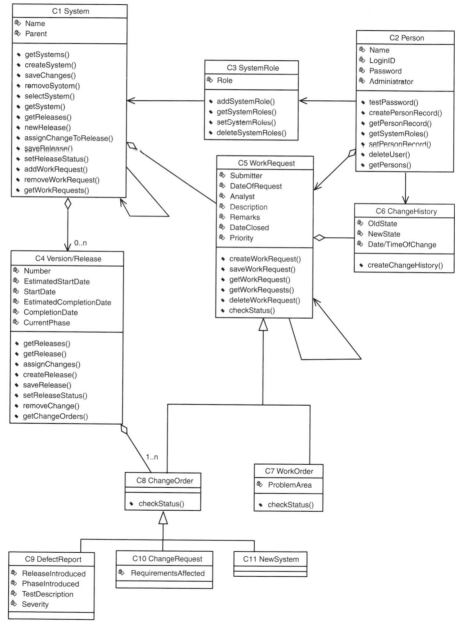

FIGURE B.1

Change Management System Class Diagram

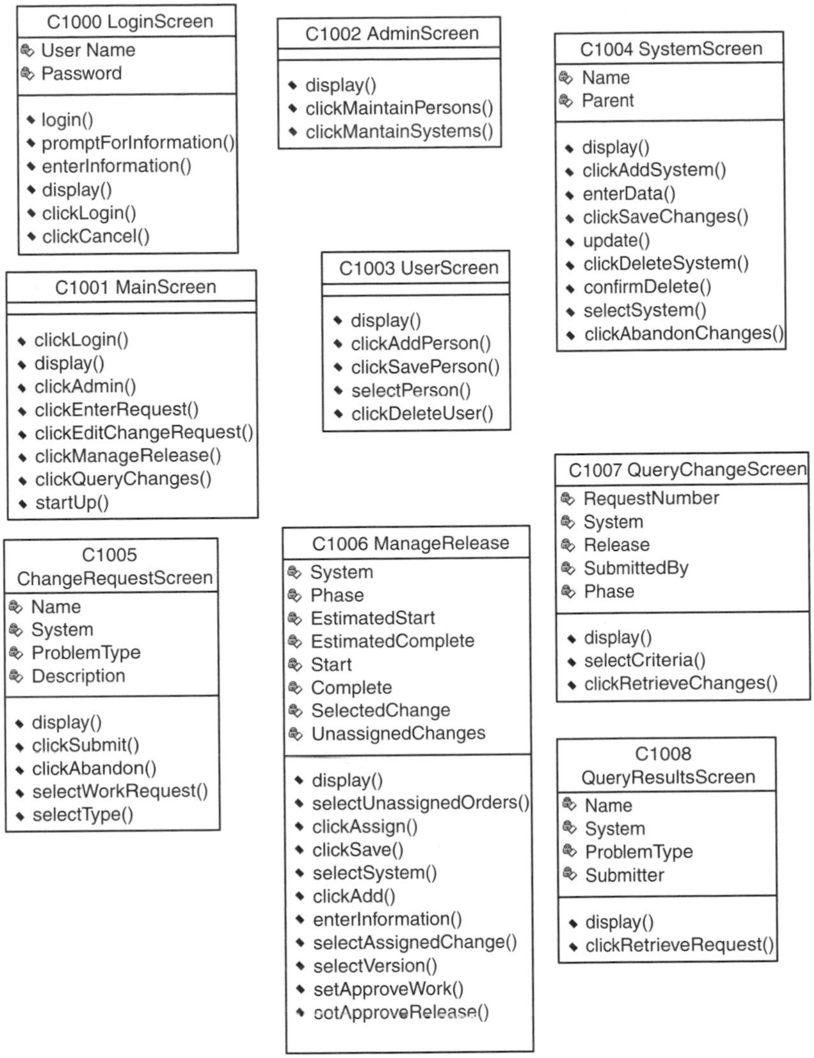

C1000 LoginScreen
- User Name
- Password

- login()
- promptForInformation()
- enterInformation()
- display()
- clickLogin()
- clickCancel()

C1002 AdminScreen
- display()
- clickMaintainPersons()
- clickMantainSystems()

C1004 SystemScreen
- Name
- Parent

- display()
- clickAddSystem()
- enterData()
- clickSaveChanges()
- update()
- clickDeleteSystem()
- confirmDelete()
- selectSystem()
- clickAbandonChanges()

C1001 MainScreen
- clickLogin()
- display()
- clickAdmin()
- clickEnterRequest()
- clickEditChangeRequest()
- clickManageRelease()
- clickQueryChanges()
- startUp()

C1003 UserScreen
- display()
- clickAddPerson()
- clickSavePerson()
- selectPerson()
- clickDeleteUser()

C1007 QueryChangeScreen
- RequestNumber
- System
- Release
- SubmittedBy
- Phase

- display()
- selectCriteria()
- clickRetrieveChanges()

C1005 ChangeRequestScreen
- Name
- System
- ProblemType
- Description

- display()
- clickSubmit()
- clickAbandon()
- selectWorkRequest()
- selectType()

C1006 ManageRelease
- System
- Phase
- EstimatedStart
- EstimatedComplete
- Start
- Complete
- SelectedChange
- UnassignedChanges

- display()
- selectUnassignedOrders()
- clickAssign()
- clickSave()
- selectSystem()
- clickAdd()
- enterInformation()
- selectAssignedChange()
- selectVersion()
- setApproveWork()
- setApproveRelease()

C1008 QueryResultsScreen
- Name
- System
- ProblemType
- Submitter

- display()
- clickRetrieveRequest()

FIGURE B.2
Change Management System Graphical User Interface Classes

Change Management System State Diagrams

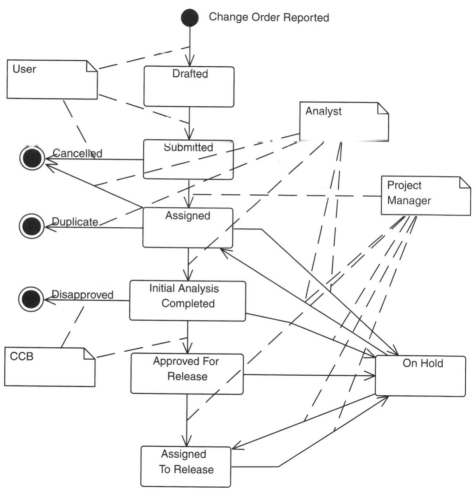

FIGURE B.3
Change Order State Transition Diagram

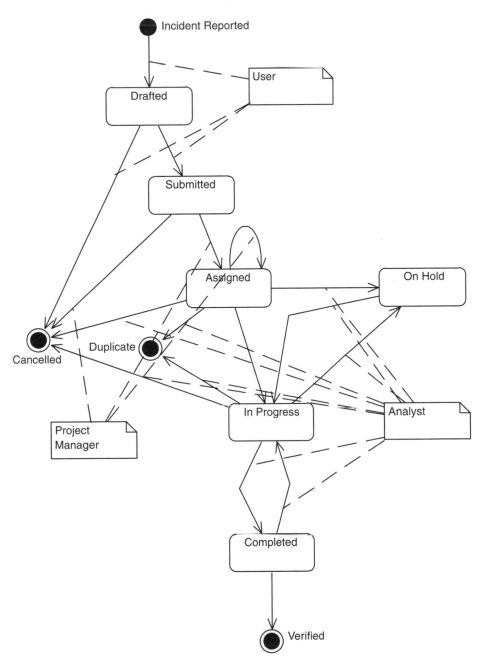

FIGURE B.4
Work Order State Transition Diagram

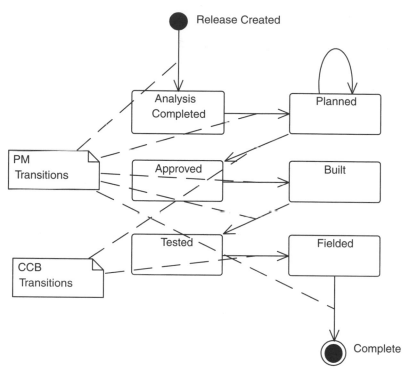

FIGURE B.5
Release State Transition Diagram

Change Management
Software Requirements Specification _____

Software Requirements Specification

for the

Change Management System

Version 1

Prepared by R. Abreo and D. Windle

19 February 2002

Table of Contents

TABLE B.2
Revision History

Name	Date	Reason for Change	Version
R. Abreo, D. Windle	4/29/01	Initial Release	1.0.1

1. Introduction

1.1. Purpose

This document will define all system requirements for the Change Management System. The intended audience for the SRS includes the users, developers, and testers.

1.2. Scope

The Change Management System will provide users with the ability to enter and manage trouble requests and software requests to include request for software systems, enhancement request, and defect reports. The Change Management System will allow any software request to be included in a version of the software. This allows all changes associated with a version to be managed as a group.

1.3. Definitions, Acronyms, and Abbreviations

Term	Definition
Baseline	An established set of artifacts that together represent a given version of a system.
Change Order	A generic term used to refer to any request that will require software baselines to be modified or created.
Change Request	A request to change an existing version of a system.
Defect Report	A report that indicates a system is not behaving as specified.
Release	An executable version of a system and all artifacts associated with the version
System	The hardware and software provided to a customer to meet the customer's needs.

Term	Definition
System Role	A named set of permissions that may be exercised for a given system.
Version	A specific set of functionality in a given system.
Work Order	A user-reported issue that will not require baseline changes to the software system.
Work Request	The generic name applied to any request submitted for a system. This includes Work Orders, Defect Reports, Change Requests, and requests for new systems.

1.4. References

- IEEE Standards "Software Engineering, Volume Two, Process Standards," Std 830-1998, 1999 Edition.
- *The Unified Development Process*, I. Jacobson, G. Booch, J. Rumbaugh, January 1999.
- *Software Engineering—A Practitioner's Approach*, Roger S. Pressman, 1992.

1.5. Overview

This document will describe all the specific requirements for the Change Management System. All nonfunctional requirements will be defined in statement form. Each nonfunctional requirement will be measurable or be able to be checked off as met or not met. Software requirements are described in terms of the entities, or classes, that make up the system. The software requirements were gathered and analyzed with an object-oriented approach coupled with a screen prototyping and storyboarding approach. The artifacts developed through this process will be maintained as attachments to this document. These artifacts include the Use Case Models, Use Case Specifications, Analysis Class Diagram, Sequence Diagrams, and the screen prototypes/storyboards.

2. Overall Description

2.1. Product Perspective

The Change Management System provides the users a tool that allows each request to be managed to closure. In addition, the system provides an effective tool for planning and managing versions of the system.

2.1.1. System interfaces

No external system interfaces are required.

2.1.2. User interfaces

The user interface shall require a distributed environment to allow users in various physical locations to access the system. Specific information about the Graphical User Interface is included in paragraph 3.1.1 below.

2.1.3. Hardware interfaces

No hardware interfaces are required.

2.1.4. Software interfaces

No current software interfaces are required.

2.1.5. Communications interfaces

No communications interfaces are required.

2.1.6. Memory

No specific memory requirements have been specified.

2.1.7. Operations

There are no specific operational requirements.

2.1.8. Site adaptation requirements

There are no specific site adaptation requirements.

2.2. Product Functions

The products major functions are to:

- Allow users to submit Work Request.
- Allow Analyst to be assigned to and process Work Request.

- Allow Project Manager to manage Work Request and Versions of Systems.
- Allow CCB representatives to approve and manage Versions of Systems.
- Allow effective administration of the system.

2.3. User Characteristics

The users are trained software professionals that manage work requests and the requesters of work for systems. Each user profile is specified below.

2.3.1. User

The term User is generic to describe anyone who may submit a work request.

2.3.2. Analyst

An Analyst is a software professional assigned to work a given work request.

2.3.3. Project Manager

A Project Manager is the person responsible for a version of a system.

2.3.4. Change Control Board

The CCB represents the group that approves work requests to go forward and approves versions of the system for work and deployment.

2.3.5. Administrator

The Administrator is responsible for granting access to people for a given role on a given system.

2.4. Constraints

No constraints have been noted for the system.

2.5. Assumptions and Dependencies

None noted.

2.6. Apportioning of Requirements

The complete application will be built in a single release.

3. Specific Requirements

Section 3 of this SRS shall use the A.4 Template of the IEEE standard. One modification has been made to this template. The messages are included as references in the functions specified and are not included at the end of class definitions.

3.1. External Interface Requirements

This section specifies each external interface the system will require.

3.1.1. Graphical User Interfaces

The GUI system will provide users with easy access to needed functions. Below are the specific requirements.

3.1.1.1. RN C1000, Login Screen

The Login Screen shall allow the user to authenticate with the system. The system shall ensure the user is assigned to the correct access to all appropriate systems.

3.1.1.1.1. RN C1000-A1, User Name   The user shall be allowed to enter between 1 and 10 characters long, inclusively.

3.1.1.1.2 RN C1000-A2, Password   The user shall be allowed to enter between 1 and 10 characters long, inclusively. The system shall echo the "*" character to the screen whenever the user enters a character.

3.1.1.1.3. RN C1000-M1, Display   The system shall display the Login screen whenever the application is started.

3.1.1.1.4. RN C1000-M2, Click Login   The system shall determine what person is attempting to log in (see paragraph RN C2-M3, Get Person Record). If the given user ID does not match a known user ID, the system shall display the screen (see paragraph RN C1000-M1, Display) along with the error. If the given person is found, the system shall ensure that the given password matches the password of the record (see paragraph RN C2-M1, Test Password). If the given password does not match the password in the record, the system shall display the screen (see paragraph RN C1000-M1, Display) along with the error. Otherwise, the system shall display the main screen (see paragraph RN C1001-M2, Display).

3.1.1.1.5. RN C1000-M3, Click Cancel   The system shall stop the application.

3.1.1.2. RN C1001, Main Screen

The Main Screen shall provide users the ability to navigate the system screens.

31.1.2.1. RN C1001-M1, Startup   The system shall require the user to log in to the system (see paragraph RN C1000-M1, Display).

3.1.1.2.2. RN C1001-M2, Display   The system shall display the main screen.

3.1.1.2.3. RN C1001-M3, Click Admin   If the User is an Administrator (see paragraph RN C2-M8, Is Administrator), the system shall display the Admin screen (see paragraph RN C1002-M1, Display).

3.1.1.2.4. RN C1001-M4, Click Enter Request   The system shall display the Change Request Screen (see paragraph RN C1005-M1, Display).

3.1.1.2.5. RN C1001-M5, Click Edit Change Request   The system shall display the Change Request Screen (see paragraph RN C1005-M1, Display).

3.1.1.2.6. RN C1001-M6, Click Manage Release   The system shall display the Manage Release Screen (see paragraph RN C1006-M1, Display).

3.1.1.2.7. RN C1001-M7 Click Query Changes   The system shall display the Query Changes Screen (see paragraph RN C1007-M1, Display)

3.1.1.3. RN C1002, Admin Screen

The Admin Screen shall provide navigation to the Persons screen and the Systems screen.

3.1.1.3.1. RN C1002-M1, Display   The system shall display the Admin screen.

3.1.1.3.2. RN C1002-M2, Click Maintain Persons   The system shall display the Person screen (see paragraph RN C1003-M1, Display).

3.1.1.3.3. RN C1002-M3, Click Maintain Systems   The system shall display the System screen (see paragraph 3.1.1.5.3. RN C1004-M1, Display).

3.1.1.4. RN C1003, User Screen

The User Screen shall allow administrators to maintain information about users of the system.

3.1.1.4.1. RN C1003-A1, Name   This text field shall display the name field of the record. The user shall be allowed to enter from 0 to 20 alphabetical characters.

3.1.1.4.2. RN C1003-A2, User Identifier   This text field shall display the User Identifier field of the record. The user shall be allowed to enter from 0 to 10 alphabetical characters.

3.1.1.4.3. RN C1003-A3, Password   This text field shall display the password field of the record. The user shall be allowed to enter from 0 to 20 alphabetical characters.

3.1.1.4.4. RN C1003-A4, E-Mail   This text field shall display the e-mail address field of the record. The user shall be allowed to enter from 0 to 50 alphanumeric characters and allow the characters "." and "@".

3.1.1.4.5. RN C1003-A5, Administrator   This Boolean field shall display true if the record is for an administrator. Otherwise, false shall be displayed. The user shall be allowed to set the indicator to true or false.

3.1.1.4.6. RN C1003-A6, Available Systems   The system shall display a list of systems for which the user has not been assigned a role. The system shall allow the user to select a system from the list for role assignment.

3.1.1.4.7. RN C1003-A7, Assigned Systems   The system shall display a list of systems for which the user has already been assigned a role. The system shall allow the user to select a system and remove access for the given person.

3.1.1.4.8. RN C1003-A8, System Role   The system shall present a list of roles to which the given user may be assigned for the selected system.

3.1.1.4.9. RN C1003-M1, Display   The system shall retrieve all person records (see paragraph RN C2-M7, Get Persons). The system shall set the person to the first person in the list. The system shall retrieve the given person (see paragraph RN C2-M3, Get Person Record). The system shall determine all systems that are associated with the given person (see paragraph

RN C3-M2, Get System Roles) and retrieve the associated systems (see paragraph RN C1-M1, Get Systems). The system shall retrieve all systems not associated with the person (see paragraph RN C1-M1, Get Systems).

3.1.1.4.10. RN C1003-M2, Click Add Person The system shall clear all fields on the screen. The system shall move all Systems to the available list.

3.1.1.4.11. RN C1003-M3, Click Save Person If the action Person does not exist, the system shall create a new Person (see paragraph RN C2-M2, Create Person Record). The system shall save all person information to Person (see paragraph RN C2-M5, Set Person Record). The system shall then display the Person.

3.1.1.4.12. RN C1003-M4, Select Person The system shall retrieve the given person (see paragraph RN C2-M3, Get Person Record). The system shall determine all systems that are associated with the given person (see paragraph RN C2-M4, Get System Roles) and retrieve the associated systems (see paragraph RN C1-M1, Get Systems). The system shall retrieve all systems not associated with the person (see paragraph RN C1-M1, Get Systems).

3.1.1.4.13. RN C1003-M5, Click Delete User The system shall delete the user record (see paragraph RN C2-M6, Delete User). The system shall select the next person (see paragraph RN C1003-M4, Select Person) for display.

3.1.1.5. RN C1004, System Screen

The System Screen shall allow the administrator to maintain specific information for systems.

3.1.1.5.1. RN C1004-A1, Name This text field shall display the name field of the record. The user shall be allowed to enter from 0 to 20 alphabetical characters.

3.1.1.5.2. RN C1004-A2, Parent The system shall present a list of all systems, except the given system. The system shall allow the user to select the parent system from the given list.

3.1.1.5.3. RN C1004-M1, Display The system shall retrieve all systems available (see paragraph RN C1-M1, Get Systems). The system shall determine the parent of the first System in the list (see paragraph RN C1-M12,

Get Parent) and display the Parent System. All systems except the System currently being displayed and the Parent System shall be placed in the available Parents list.

3.1.1.5.4. RN C1004-M2, Click Add System   The system shall set the System Name and System Parent attributes to blank.

3.1.1.5.5. RN C1004-M3, Click Save Changes   If the action is creating a new System, the system shall create the new System (see paragraph RN C1-M2, Create System). The system shall save the system (see paragraph RN C1-M3, Save System). The system shall select the System for display (see paragraph RN C1004-M5, Select System).

3.1.1.5.6. RN C1004-M4, Click Delete System   The system shall delete the System (see paragraph 3.2.1.6. RN C1-M4, Remove System). The system shall select the next System in the list (see paragraph RN C1004-M5, Select System) for display.

3.1.1.5.7. RN C1004-M5, Select System   The system shall retrieve the selected system (see paragraph RN C1-M6, Get System). The system shall determine the parent of the first System in the list (see paragraph RN C1-M12, Get Parent) and display the Parent System. All systems except the System currently being displayed and the Parent System shall be placed in the available Systems list and the available Parents list.

3.1.1.5.8. RN C1004-M6, Click Abandon Changes   The system shall select the System at the top of the available Systems list (see paragraph RN C1004-M5, Select System).

3.1.1.6. RN C1005, Change Request Screen

The Change Request Screen shall allow the user to create and maintain change request.

3.1.1.6.1. RN C1005-A1, Name   This text field shall display the name field of the record. The user shall be allowed to enter from 0 to 20 alphabetical characters.

3.1.1.6.2. RN C1005-A2, System   The system shall present a list of all systems. The system shall allow the user to select the parent system from the given list.

3.1.1.6.3. RN C1005-A3, Problem Type   The system shall present a list of all problem types. The system shall allow the user to select the problem type from the given list.

Note: The allowable problem types are Change Request, New System, Defect Report, and Work Order.

3.1.1.6.4. RN C1005-A4, Description   The system shall present the description of the request. The system shall allow the user to enter from 0 to 2048 characters to describe the request.

3.1.1.6.5. RN C1005-M1, Display   If a Work Request was given, the system shall retrieve the Work Request (see paragraph RN C5-M3, Get Work Request). The system shall retrieve all available systems (see paragraph RN C1-M1, Get Systems) and place them into a list. If a Work Request was given, the assigned System shall be selected. Otherwise, the system shall select the first System in the list. The system shall retrieve all Releases associated with the given system (see paragraph RN C1-M7, Get Releases) and place them into a list. If a Work Request was given, the assigned Release shall be selected. Otherwise, the system shall select the first Release in the list.

3.1.1.6.6. RN C1005-M2, Click Submit   If this action is creating a new Work Request, the system shall create a new Work Request of the appropriate type (see paragraph RN C5-M1, Create Work Request). The system shall ensure the saving of the Work Request (see paragraph RN C5-M2, Save Work Request). If no error is returned, the system shall display the Work Request Screen with the Work Request (see paragraph RN C1005-M1, Display). If an error is returned, the system shall display the error along with the unsaved information.

3.1.1.6.7. RN C1005-M3, Click Abandon   The system shall abandon the action and display the Change Request Screen (see paragraph RN C1005-M1, Display).

3.1.1.6.8. RN C1005-M4, Select Change Request   The system shall display the Change Request Screen with the given Work Request (see paragraph RN C1005-M1, Display).

3.1.1.6.9. RN C1005-M5, Select Type   The system shall display the only the Work Requests of the given type.

3.1.1.6.10. RN C1005-M6, Select Work Request The system shall display the Change Request Screen with the given Work Request (see paragraph RN C1005-M1, Display).

3.1.1.7. RN C1006, Manage Release

The Manage Release Screen shall allow the user to add and modify releases associated with the given system.

3.1.1.7.1. RN C1006-A1, System The system shall present a list of all available systems with the currently selected system highlighted. The system shall allow the user to select a system from the given list.

3.1.1.7.2. RN C1006-A2, Phase The system shall present a list of phases with the currently selected phase highlighted. The system shall allow the user to select Requirements, Design, Code, Test, Deployment, or Completed for the phase.

3.1.1.7.3. RN C1006-A3, Estimated Start The system shall present the estimated start date. The system shall allow the user to enter an estimated start date.

3.1.1.7.4. RN C1006-A4, Estimated Complete The system shall present the estimated completion date. The system shall allow the user to enter an estimated completion date.

3.1.1.7.5. RN C1006-A5, Start The system shall present the start date. The system shall allow the user to enter a start date.

3.1.1.7.6. RN C1006-A6, Complete The system shall present the completed date. The system shall allow the user to enter a completed date.

3.1.1.7.7. RN C1006-A7, Selected Changes The system shall present a list of all change orders currently associated with the release. The system shall allow the user to select a change from the given list and request that it be moved to the Unassigned List.

3.1.1.7.8. RN C1006-A8, Unassigned Changes The system shall present a list of all change orders currently associated with the system but not associated with any release. The system shall allow the user to select a change from the given list and request that it be moved to the Assigned List.

3.1.1.7.9. RN C1006-M1, Display The system shall retrieve all Systems (see paragraph RN C1-M1, Get Systems) for which the user plays the role of

Project Manager or CCB (see paragraph RN C3-M2, Get System Roles) and place them into a list. If no System was given, the system shall select the first System in the list as the active System. The system shall retrieve all Releases for the active System (see paragraph RN C1-M7, Get Releases) and place them into a list. If no Release was given, the system shall set the first Release as the active Release. The system shall retrieve all Change Request associated with the active Release (see paragraph RN C4-M9, Get Change Orders) and place them into a list. The system shall retrieve all Change Orders associated with the System but not currently assigned to any Release (see paragraph RN C1-M15, Get Work Requests).

3.1.1.7.10. RN C1006-M2, Select Unassigned Orders The system shall make the currently selected unassigned Change Order the active Change Order for assignment.

3.1.1.7.11. RN C1006-M3, Click Assign The system shall assign the active, unassigned Change Order to the current Release (see paragraph RN C1-M9, Assign Change to Release).

3.1.1.7.12. RN C1006-M4, Click Save The system shall save changes to the version (see paragraph RN C1-M10, Save Release).

3.1.1.7.13. RN C1006-M5, Select System The system shall display the Manage Release Screen with the selected System (see paragraph RN C1006-M1, Display).

3.1.1.7.14. RN C1006-M6, Click Add The system shall set all fields blank. The system shall display all unassigned Change Orders in a list format.

3.1.1.7.15. RN C1006-M7, Select Assigned Change The system shall make the currently selected assigned Change Order the active Change Order for assignment.

3.1.1.7.16. RN C1006-M8, Select Version The system shall display the Manage Release Screen with the current System and selected Release (see paragraph RN C1006-M1, Display).

3.1.1.7.17. RN C1006-M9, Set Approve Work If the user has the role of CCB (see paragraph RN C3-M2, Get System Roles) for the current system, the system shall set the Release for Work for the current Release on the screen.

3.1.1.7.18. RN C1006-M10, Set Approve Release   If the user has the role of CCB (see paragraph RN C3-M2, Get System Roles) for the current system, the system shall set the Approved for Release to true for the current Release on the screen.

3.1.1.8. RN C1007, Query Change Screen

The Query Change Screen shall allow the user to query the system to find changes, based on different criteria.

3.1.1.8.1. RN C1007-A1, Request Number   The system shall allow the user to enter the request number.

3.1.1.8.2. RN C1007-A2, System   The system shall present a list of all available systems. The system shall allow the user to select a system from the given list.

3.1.1.8.3. RN C1007-A3, Release   The system shall present a list of all available releases associated with the selected system. The system shall allow the user to select a release from the given list.

3.1.1.8.4. RN C1007-A4, Submitted By   The system shall present a list of all users that have entered a work request. The system shall allow the user to select a user from the given list.

3.1.1.8.5. RN C1007-A5, Phase   The system shall present a list of all phases a work order may be in. The system shall allow the user to select a phase from the given list.

3.1.1.8.6. RN C1007-M1, Display   The system shall retrieve all Systems (see paragraph RN C1-M1, Get Systems) and place them into a list. The system shall set the first System in the list to the active System. The system shall retrieve all Releases for the active System (see paragraph RN C1-M7, Get Releases) and place them into a list. The system retrieve all Persons that have submitted a change request (see paragraph RN C2-M7, Get Persons) and place them into a list. The system shall populate the list for Phase of Change.

3.1.1.8.7. RN C1007-M2, Select Criteria   The system shall include all selections made by the user into the criteria used to retrieve changes.

3.1.1.8.8. RN C1007-M3, Click Retrieve Changes   The system shall retrieve all changes that meet the given criteria (see paragraph RN C5-M4,

Get Work Requests). The system shall display the Query Results Screen (see paragraph RN C1008-M1, Display).

3.1.1.9. RN C1008, Query Results Screen

The Query Results Screen shall present the user with all work requests that were returned from a given query. The system shall allow the user to select a work request.

   3.1.1.9.1. RN C1008-A1, Name   The system shall present the name of each Work Request returned from the query.

   3.1.1.9.2. RN C1008-A2, System   The system shall present the System with which each Work Request that is returned is associated.

   3.1.1.9.3. RN C1008-A3, Problem Type   The system shall present the problem type of each Work Request returned from the query.

   3.1.1.9.4. RN C1008-A4, Submitter   The system shall present the name of the user that submitted the Work Request for each of the Work Requests returned from the query.

   3.1.1.9.5. RN C1008-M1, Display   The system shall display all the given Work Requests.

   3.1.1.9.6. RN C1008-M2, Click Retrieve Request   The system shall display the Change Request Screen with the given Work Request (see paragraph RN C1005-M1, Display).

3.1.2. Hardware interfaces

No specialized interfaces are required.

3.1.3. Software interfaces

No software interfaces are required.

3.1.4. Communications interfaces

No communications interfaces are required.

3.2. Classes/Objects

This section specifies all classes in the business domain for the system.

3.2.1. RN C1, System

The System class represents the software systems that will be managed by the Change Management System. The system class will include a collection of Versions and Work Request.

3.2.1.1. RN C1-A1, Name

The Change Management System shall maintain the name of each system managed. The Name shall be inclusively between 1 and 20 alphabetical characters long and must be unique to the system.

3.2.1.2. RN C1-A2, Parent

The System shall represent a subsystem to another system managed by the Change Management System. In this case, the system shall maintain a reference to the parent system.

3.2.1.3. RN C1-M1, Get Systems

The system shall return the set of systems that meet the criteria given.

3.2.1.4. RN C1-M2, Create System

The system shall create the System object.

3.2.1.5. RN C1-M3, Save System

The system shall save the System.

3.2.1.6. RN C1-M4, Remove System

The system shall determine Persons related to the system (see paragraph RN C3-M2, Get System Roles) and remove each of those relationships (see paragraph RN C3-M4, Delete System Role). The system shall retrieve any Work Request related to the System (see paragraph RN C5-M4, Get Work Requests) and delete each request (see paragraph RN C5-M5, Delete Work Requests). The system shall retrieve any related Versions (see paragraph RN C4-M1, Get Releases) and delete each version (see paragraph RN C4-M7, Delete Release).

3.2.1.7. RN C1-M5, Select System

The system shall return the selected System.

3.2.1.8. RN C1-M6, Get System

The system shall return the requested System.

3.2.1.9. RN C1-M7, Get Releases

The system shall return all Releases associated with the given System that match the given criteria.

3.2.1.10. RN C1-M8, New Release

The system shall create a new Release (see paragraph RN C4-M4, Create Release).

3.2.1.11. RN C1-M9, Assign Change to Release

The system shall add the Work Request to the given Release (see paragraph RN C4-M3, Assign Changes).

3.2.1.12. RN C1-M10, Save Release

If the Release is new, the system shall create a Release (see paragraph RN C4-M4, Create Release). The system shall save all given values (see paragraph RN C4-M5, Save Release). The system shall ensure that all assigned Change Orders are assigned to the Release (see paragraph RN C4-M3, Assign Changes). If the status has changed, the system shall set the Release status (see paragraph RN C1-M11, Set Release Status).

3.2.1.13. RN C1-M11, Set Release Status

The system shall set the Release status (see paragraph RN C4-M6, Set Release Status).

3.2.1.14. RN C1-M12, Get Parent

The system shall return the Parent of the System.

3.2.1.15. RN C1-M13, Add Work Request

The system shall add the Work Request to the collection of Work Request for the system. If the Work Request references a Release, the system shall add the Work Request to the release (see paragraph RN C1-M9, Assign Change to Release).

3.2.1.16. RN C1-M14, Remove Work Request

The system shall remove the Work Request from the collection of Work Request for the system. If the Work Request references a Release, the system shall remove the Work Request to the release (see paragraph RN C4-M8, Remove Change Order).

3.2.1.17. RN C1-M15, Get Work Requests

The system shall return all Work Requests assigned to the System that match the given criteria.

3.2.2. RN C2, Person

The Person class represents the users of the Change Management System. The Person class shall include a collection of System Roles that specify a specific role for a specific system. The Person class shall be related to zero or more Work Requests.

3.2.2.1. RN C2-A1, Name

The system shall maintain the name of the person. The name will be inclusively between 1 and 20 alphabetical characters long.

3.2.2.2. RN C2-A2, Login Identifier

The system shall maintain the user ID or login ID for the person. The login ID shall be inclusively between 1 and 10 alphanumeric characters long and must be unique to the system.

3.2.2.3. RN C2-A3, Password

The system shall maintain the password for the person. The password shall be inclusively between 1 and 10 alphanumeric characters long.

3.2.2.4. RN C2-A4, Administrator

The system shall maintain an indicator to determine if the person is an Administrator. The indicator shall be true or false.

3.2.2.5. RN C2-M1, Test Password

The system shall return true if the given password matches the Password.

3.2.2.6. RN C2-M2, Create Person Record

The system shall create a new Person.

3.2.2.7. RN C2-M3, Get Person Record

The system shall determine whether the given user ID can be found. If the user ID is found, the system shall return the Person object for the given user ID. If the user ID cannot be found, the system shall return nothing.

3.2.2.8. RN C2-M4, Get System Roles

The system shall return each System associated with the Person and the Role the Person plays on the given System.

3.2.2.9. RN C2-M5, Set Person Record

The system shall set all attributes to the given values. The system shall delete all System Roles (see paragraph RN C3-M4, Delete System Role). The system shall add each System Role for the Person (see paragraph RN C3-M1, Add System Role).

3.2.2.10. RN C2-M6, Delete User

The system shall determine each System the Person is associated with (see paragraph RN C2-M4, Get System Roles) and remove each System Role (see paragraph RN C3-M4, Delete System Role). The system shall then remove the Person.

3.2.2.11. RN C2-M7, Get Persons

The system shall return all Person records.

3.2.2.12. RN C2-M8, Is Administrator

The system shall return true if the Person is an Administrator. Otherwise, the system shall return false.

3.2.3. RN C3, System Role

The System Role class represents the relationship between a Person object and a System object. The system Role object shall include a reference to a person object and a reference to a system object.

3.2.3.1. RN C3-A1, Role

The system shall maintain an enumerated value to indicate the role a person plays for a given system. The role shall be User, Analyst, Project Manager, or CCB.

3.2.3.2. RN C3-M1, Add System Role

The system shall set the given role to the Role attribute and record the Person and the related System.

3.2.3.3. RN C3-M2, Get System Roles

The system shall return all system roles for the given user ID.

3.2.3.4. RN C3-M3, Set System Roles

The system shall set the System Role to the given roles.

3.2.3.5. RN C3-M4, Delete System Role

The system shall delete the System Role.

3.2.4. RN C4, Version/Release

The Version/Release class represents a version or release of a software system. A Version/Release object shall always be assigned to exactly one System object. The Version/Release object shall have a collection of zero to many Change Order objects.

3.2.4.1. RN C4-A1, Number

The system shall maintain a release number for each Version/Release. The number shall be 6 numeric characters long.

3.2.4.2. RN C4-A2, Estimated Start Date

The system shall maintain a date value to represent the Estimated Start Date.

3.2.4.3. RN C4-A3, Start Date

The system shall maintain a date value to represent the Start Date.

3.2.4.4. RN C4-A4, Estimated Completion Date

The system shall maintain a date value to represent the Estimated Completion Date.

3.2.4.5. RN C4-A5, Completion Date

The system shall maintain a date value to represent the Completion Date.

3.2.4.6. RN C4-A6, Current Phase

The system shall maintain an enumerated value to indicate the current phase of the release. The system shall allow the values of Created, Analysis Complete, Planned, Approved, Built, Tested, Fielded, or Complete.

3.2.4.7. RN C4-M1, Get Releases

The system shall return all Releases that match the given criteria.

3.2.4.8. RN C4-M2, Get Release

The system shall return the identified Release. If the Release cannot be found, the system shall return nothing.

3.2.4.9. RN C4-M3, Assign Changes

The system shall assign the given Change Order to the Release.

3.2.4.10. RN C4-M4, Create Release

The system shall create a new Release.

3.2.4.11. RN C4-M5, Save Release

The system shall save all values of the Release.

3.2.4.12. RN C4-M6, Set Release Status

The system shall set the Release Status to the given value.

3.2.4.13. RN C4-M7, Delete Release

The system shall delete the Release.

3.2.4.14. RN C4-M8, Remove Change Order

The system shall remove the given Change Order from the collection of Change Requests for the Release.

3.2.4.15. RN C4-M9, Get Change Orders

The system shall return all Change Orders associated with the Release.

3.2.5. RN C5, Work Request

The Work Request class represents requests to perform some work for the requestor. This class is an abstract class and serves as the base class for Work Order and Change Order. The Work Request class shall have a collection of Work History objects to record all changes.

3.2.5.1. RN C5-A1, Submitter

The system shall maintain the identifier of the person that submitted the request.

3.2.5.2. RN C5-A2, Date Of Request

The system shall maintain a date value to represent the date the request was made.

3.2.5.3. RN C5-A3, Analyst

The system shall maintain the identifier of the person assigned to the request.

3.2.5.4. RN C5-A4, Description

The system shall maintain a string to represent the description of the request. The system shall allow the value to be 0 to 2048 characters long.

3.2.5.5. RN C5-A5, Remarks

The system shall maintain a string to represent the remarks about the request. The system shall allow the value to be 0 to 2048 characters long.

3.2.5.6. RN C5-A6, Date Closed

The system shall maintain a date value to represent date the request was closed.

3.2.5.7. RN C5-A7, Priority

The system shall maintain an integer value between 1 and 6 to represent the priority of the request.

3.2.5.8. RN C5-M1, Create Work Request

The system shall create the Work Request of the appropriate type and create a Change History to record the event (see paragraph RN C6-M1, Create Change History) The system shall add the Work Request to the appropriate system (see paragraph RN C1-M12, Get Parent).

3.2.5.9. RN C5-M2, Save Work Request

The system shall save the Work Request information. If the status has changed, the system shall ensure the status change is allowed (see paragraph RN C5-M6, Check Status). If an error is returned, the system returns the error to the User. If the System has changed, the system shall remove the change from the System (see paragraph RN C1-M14, Remove Work Request) and then assign the Work Request to the given System (see paragraph RN C1-M13, Add Work Request).

3.2.5.10. RN C5-M3, Get Work Request

The system shall return a Work Request object of the appropriate type for the given Work Request ID. If the Work Request ID could not be found, the system shall return null.

3.2.5.11. RN C5-M4, Get Work Requests

The system shall return the Work Request that matches the given criteria.

3.2.5.12. RN C5-M5, Delete Work Requests

The system shall delete the Work Request.

3.2.5.13. RN C5-M6, Check Status

If the Work Request is a Work Order, the system shall check the status of the Work Order (see paragraph RN C7-M1, Check Status). Otherwise, the system shall check the status of the Change Order (see paragraph RN C8-M1, Check Status). If no errors are returned, the system shall create a Change History (see paragraph RN C6-M1, Create Change History).

3.2.6. RN C6, Change History

The Change History class represents the transition of a Work Request or Version/Release.

3.2.6.1. RN C6-A1, Old State

The system shall maintain the state of the artifact before the change. The system shall allow the values to be Assigned, Cancelled, Completed, Drafted, Duplicate, Incident Reported, In Progress, On Hold, Submitted, Verified, Approved for Release, Assigned to Release, Change Order Reported, or Initial Analysis Complete.

3.2.6.2. RN C6-A2, New State

The system shall maintain the state of the artifact after the change is applied.

3.2.6.3. RN C6-A3, Date Time Of Change

The system shall maintain a date and time value to represent date and time the change occurred.

3.2.6.4. RN C6-M1, Create Change History

The system shall create a Change History and add the Old State and New State to the values given. The system shall set the Date and Time to the current system date and time.

3.2.7. RN C7, Work Order

The Work Order class represents a request to perform some work for the requestor. The work does not require a change to a software baseline.

3.2.7.1. RN C7-A1, Problem Area

The system shall maintain the problem area requiring work. The allowable values are System Configuration, Software Installation, and User Error.

3.2.7.2. RN C7-M1, Check Status

The system shall ensure that the given person may change the status from the old status to the new status. Otherwise, the system shall return the error "Change Not Allowed."

a. If the given Role is "User," the system shall ensure the given status change is

    a.1. None to "Drafted" or

    a.2. "Drafted" to "Submitted" or

    a.3. "Drafted" to "Cancelled."

b. If the given Role is "Analyst," the system shall ensure the given status change is

    b.1. "Assigned" to "Cancelled" or

    b.2. "Assigned" to "On Hold" or

    b.3. "Assigned" to "Duplicate" or

    b.4. "Assigned" to "In Progress" or

    b.5. "On Hold" to "In Progress" or

    b.6. "In Progress" to "On Hold" or

    b.7. "InProgress" to "Duplicate" or

    b.8. "InProgress" to "Cancelled" or

    b.9. "InProgress" to "Complete."

c. If the given Role is "Project Manager," the system shall ensure the given status change is

    c.1. "Submitted" to "Cancelled" or

    c.2. "Submitted" to "Assigned" or

    c.3. "Assigned" to "Assigned" or

    c.4. "Complete" to "Verified."

3.2.8. RN C8, Change Order

The Change Order class represents a request to perform some work for the requestor. The work does require a change to software baseline. This class is an abstract class and serves as the base class for Defect Reports, Change Request, and New System.

3.2.8.1. RN C8-M1, Check Status

The system shall ensure that the given person may change the status from the old status to the new status. Otherwise, the system will return the error "Change Not Allowed."

a. If the given Role is "User," the system shall ensure that the given status change is

    a.1. None to "Drafted" or

    a.2. "Drafted" to "Submitted" or

a.3. "Submitted" to "Cancelled."

b. If the given Role is "Analyst," the system shall ensure that the given status change is

b.1. "Assigned" to "Cancelled" or

b.2. "Assigned" to "On Hold" or

b.3. "Assigned" to "Duplicate" or

b.4. "Assigned" to "Initial Analysis Complete" or

b.5. "On Hold" to "Assigned."

c. If the given Role is "Project Manager," the system shall ensure that the given status change is

c.1. "Submitted" to "Assigned" or

c.2. "Assigned" to "Assigned" or

c.3. "Assigned" to "On Hold" or

c.4. "On Hold" to "Assigned" or

c.5. "On Hold" to "Assigned to Release" or

c.6. "Initial Analysis Completed" to "On Hold" or

c.7. "Approved For Release" to "On Hold" or

c.8. "Approved For Release" to "Assigned To Release" or

c.9. "Assigned To Release" to "On Hold."

d. If the given Role is "CCB," the system shall ensure that the given status change is

d.1. "Initial Analysis Complete" to "Disapproved" or

d.2. "Initial Analysis Complete" to "Approved For Release."

3.2.9. RN C9, Defect Report

The Defect Report class represents a request to correct a software system.

3.2.9.1. RN C9-A1, Release Introduced

The system shall maintain a release number to represent the release number in which the defect was introduced. The number shall be 6 numeric characters long.

3.2.9.2. RN C9-A2, Phase Introduced

The system shall maintain the phase in which the defect was introduced into the system. The allowable values are Requirements, Design, and Code.

3.2.9.3. RN C9-A3, Test Description

The system shall maintain a string to represent the test description in which the defect was discovered. The allowable values are 0 to 255 characters.

3.2.9.4. RN C9-A4, Severity

The system shall maintain the severity of the defect. The allowable values are 0, 1, 2, 3, or 4.

3.2.10. RN C10, Change Request

The Change Request class represents a request to add, modify or delete functionality from an existing system.

3.2.10.1. RN C10-A1, Requirements Affected

The system shall maintain a string to represent the requirements affected by the change. The system shall allow the value to 0 to 2048 alphabetical characters.

3.2.11. RN C11, New System

The New System class represents a request for a new software system.

3.3. Performance Requirements

The following section defines the specific requirements related to the performance of the system.

3.3.1. Transaction time

The system shall process all user requests within 10 seconds and return the appropriate screen.

3.3.2. Concurrent users

The system shall allow a minimum of 20 concurrent users without performance degradation.

3.4. Logical Database Requirements

Logical database requirements shall be taken from the attributes of all classes specified in paragraph 3.2 above. All of the above shall require persistence for all attributes specified.

3.5. Design Constraints

The application shall be designed to allow users to access all functions from a Web browser.

3.6. Standards Compliance

The Project Manager shall use IEEE standards whenever available and appropriate.

3.7. Software System Attributes

The following paragraphs define the requirements for software system attributes.

3.7.1. Reliability

The system shall have no more than one failure per calendar week.

3.7.2. Availability

The system shall be available during the working day. The working day is defined as 8:00 a.m. until 5:00 p.m. Eastern Standard Time.

3.7.3. Security

The system shall ensure that no user is allowed to modify data without proper authentication.

3.7.4. Maintainability

No specific maintainability requirements have been specified.

3.7.5. Portability

No portability requirements have been specified.

3.8. Other Requirements

No additional requirements have been specified.

Bibliography

Booch, Grady. *Object-Oriented Analysis and Design with Applications*, 2nd ed. Reading, Massachusetts: Addison-Wesley, 1994.

IEEE Std 830-1998, IEEE Recommended Practice for Software Requirements Specifications, The Institute of Electrical and Electronics Engineers, Inc., New York: 1998.

Jacobson, Ivar, Grady Booch, and James Rumbaugh. *The Unified Software Development Process*. Reading, Massachusetts: Addison-Wesley, 1999.

OMG-Unified Modeling Language Specification, v1.4. Object Management Group, Needham, Massachusetts: 2001.

Pressman, Roger S. *Software Engineering—A Practitioner's Approach*, 5th ed. New York: McGraw Hill, 1992.

Wiegers, Karl E. *Software Requirements*. Redmond, Washington: Microsoft Press, 1999.

Index

informIT